Government at Work

Government at Work

Policymaking in the Twenty-First-Century Congress

Edited by Sunil Ahuja
and Robert Dewhirst

LEXINGTON BOOKS
Lanham • Boulder • New York • London

Published by Lexington Books
An imprint of The Rowman & Littlefield Publishing Group, Inc.
4501 Forbes Boulevard, Suite 200, Lanham, Maryland 20706
www.rowman.com

Unit A, Whitacre Mews, 26-34 Stannary Street, London SE11 4AB

British Library Cataloguing in Publication Information Available

Library of Congress Cataloging-in-Publication Data

Names: Ahuja, Sunil, editor. | Dewhirst, Robert E., editor.
Title: Government at work : policymaking in the twenty-first-century Congress / edited by Sunil Ahuja and Robert Dewhirst.
Description: Lanham, Maryland : Rowman and Littlefield, 2016.
Identifiers: LCCN 2016002249 (print) | LCCN 2016006170 (ebook) | ISBN 9781498530576 (cloth : alk. paper) | ISBN 9781498530590 (pbk. : alk. paper) | ISBN 9781498530583 (Electronic)
Subjects: LCSH: Legislation--United States. | United States--Politics and government--21st century.
Classification: LCC KF4945 .G68 2016 (print) | LCC KF4945 (ebook) | DDC 342.73/057--dc23 LC record available at http://lccn.loc.gov/2016002249

∞™ The paper used in this publication meets the minimum requirements of American National Standard for Information Sciences Permanence of Paper for Printed Library Materials, ANSI/NISO Z39.48-1992.

Printed in the United States of America

Contents

Foreword

If ever there was a scholarly study of politics, policymaking, and Congress that was needed—this is it! Prolific scholars Sunil Ahuja and Robert Dewhirst have produced a welcome addition to the literature based on public policy and Congress at a time when the legislative branch is undergoing significant changes and many of these new approaches to policymaking seem to be quite troubling. Indeed, a common criticism from reporters and scholars alike is that Congress has brought about the very dysfunction that now plagues it on account of these changes.

The old saying "may you live in interesting times" certainly applies here as both a blessing and a curse for students and scholars studying public policy and the Congress. As pundits and the public alike bemoan the dysfunction in Washington, there is a vital role for students and scholars to promote better understanding of the situation and a responsibility for us all to propose solutions to the problems. From the influence of lobbyists and "big money" in politics, to shortened work schedules on the Hill and changes to the rules that govern the crafting of legislation, to hyperpartisanship and gridlock, these issues pose fascinating questions that beg to be answered.

Ahuja and Dewhirst have selected some of the most important and intriguing policy debates of the young century for inclusion in this book. The wide array of new and existing policy issues included in this volume—social, economic, education, healthcare, security, financial, and campaign—captures the nature and scope of the changes occurring in policymaking. Each policy case is easy to read yet thoroughly examined, which is testament to the skill of the scholars who have contributed to the book. Together, they have produced balanced yet lively assessments of the nuts and bolts of these critical policy debates.

Government at Work is appropriate for university courses on policymaking and Congress, and is designed to be the ideal supplemental text for these courses. It will also prove to be a valuable resource for scholars studying the topics. Now, if only our policymakers would heed the lessons in this book!

Robert P. Watson, Ph.D.
Professor of American Studies & Political Science
Lynn University

Preface

This edited volume features case studies written by a nationwide array of public policy scholars. In this volume, we emphasize the continuous and cyclical nature of American public policymaking. Its scope spans the entire policymaking process, exposing the readers to the interaction among all the major power centers, ranging from interest groups, media, courts, Congress, and the president, to the federal bureaucracy. It reveals the dynamic nature of the American policymaking system. The approach employed herein treats events, such as Congress passing a law or the Supreme Court announcing a ruling, as important *steps* in the policy process rather than as merely *ends* unto themselves.

In this volume, we focus on major legislation passed by Congress since the turn of the century. This volume features one case study per chapter, demonstrating how issues rise to the national agenda, pass through the congressional labyrinth to become public policies, are implemented by the federal bureaucracy, receive feedback from affected elements of the society, and ultimately evolve over the years. This eclectic approach is unique, heretofore lacking in books on public policy. Virtually all primary public policy texts focus on first explaining the policymaking process followed by chapters on major substantive policy areas such as health, environment, education, and so forth. These texts have been occasionally supplemented with books featuring one case study per book. This supplemental text, on the other hand, is designed to provide a number of extended case studies for faculty and students to use as examples showing policymaking in the major subject areas.

ONE

The Politics of the Policymaking Process in a Time of Hyperpartisanship

Sunil Ahuja and Robert Dewhirst

In a word, the policymaking process in the American political system must be described as "dynamic." It is a never-ending, non-static, circular endeavor. Once formulated, policies are often reformulated at various stages of their lives. This book is devoted toward illustrating the dynamism of American policymaking within a wide array of policy arenas.

Scholars have developed several models for explaining and analyzing the policymaking process. These range from David Easton's (1965) systems analysis to Frank Baumgartner and Bryan Jones's (1993) punctuated equilibria. A common thread among all these schemes is that the process is endless. Unfortunately, the continuous nature of the policymaking process can often appear to be counter-intuitive to the unlearned eye, those who follow politics from afar and only occasionally. A simplistic notion might lead one to portray the process as ending with the passage of a law creating a new program. This view sees legislators riding off into the Capitol Hill sunset, leaving the program, now firmly etched in the law books, in the capable hands of the government. The reality of the policymaking process, however, as we will show, is significantly more intricate and ongoing.

Issues pass through four common stages in the policymaking process: agenda-setting, policy formulation, implementation, and policy evaluation. Each stage is integral to the process. Each stage, moreover, is loaded with politics. Issues evolve over time from one stage to another through the policymaking process and then begin anew as the evaluation process ignites feedback from evaluators seeking to win placement of reconstituted issues back onto the policymaking agenda. The time required for an issue to pass through all these stages can vary greatly, from just a few months to several years. With this process repeated several times, an issue can "roll" through the policymaking process for decades, as many of the case studies in this book illustrate.

Our purpose in this chapter is to paint a fairly broad picture of these stages in the policymaking process. We will, somewhat explicitly, discuss what each phase is about, explicate the elements at work in each phase, and note how each affects the subsequent phase and the policymaking process as a whole. Our aim here is to identify the theoretical framework for the policymaking process in the American system. These theoretical contours form the basis for subsequent substantive chapters in which specific policies are analyzed. Our goal in this book is not so much to expound a new theory of policymaking, but rather to illustrate the policymaking process using an accumulation of theoretical knowledge developed by the scholarly community over the last several decades. Using new case studies, we show how that process is valid and reaffirm its basic tenets. In so doing, we hope that the readers will learn how policies are made and remade in a dynamic system and the continuous nature of those policies and the policymaking process. We now turn to a brief review of the process.

THE POLICYMAKING PROCESS

Making It on the Agenda

To be sure, even though technically there is no identifiable starting point for an issue, issues passing through the mosaic of the policymaking process must begin at the agenda-setting stage. This step features some issues rising above countless rivals to gain the attention of any of a number of important actors in the policymaking process. Indeed, issues must compete for placement on the agenda. There are many issues out there, but only a few receive the policymakers' attention at any moment. Historically and contemporaneously, issues for governmental attention span all aspects of life, from economic to social policy, domestic to foreign policy.

With a vast array of issues competing for public attention at any one time, issue advocates must convince political leaders that their issue should be placed on the agenda and deserves immediate consideration. The agenda thus is an unwritten and vaguely understood list of topics or issue stances, which concerned, but certainly not all, public officials believe should be addressed by policymaking institutions. American history is filled with issues that have risen to the top of the policy agenda—

medical care for the elderly, a retirement system for the elderly, basic civil and voting rights for African-Americans—which supporters maintained should receive a governmental remedy. So, at any one time, a large array of advocates are competing to gain the public's and the policymakers' attention for a favored cause or issue position.

What determines the placement of an issue on the agenda? In other words, how are agendas set? Broadly speaking, how an issue is defined goes a long ways toward determining whether or not it will be placed on the agenda. According to Roger Cobb and Charles Elder (1983, 96–102), the basic characteristics of issue definition include (1) the degree of specificity, (2) the scope of social significance, (3) the extent of temporal relevance, (4) the degree of complexity, and (5) the degree of categorical precedence (the extent to which it is a routine rather than an extraordinary matter). The degree to which the participants are able to use these traits to their benefit, the better off they will be. Above all else, however, an issue must be salient to reach the agenda (Cobb and Elder 1983, 103). The saliency of an issue might result from either immediate or long-term conditions. On the one hand, dramatic events, such as an assassination or a mass shooting in a restaurant, might lead to governmental action, such as passing gun control legislation. On the other hand, continued public demonstrations, replete with extensive news media coverage, might compel a reluctant Congress to pass important civil and voting rights legislation.

In this process, groups are known to have differential access to the political system and differential responsiveness to their agenda items by the decision-makers. These differential factors are based largely upon unequal resources available to the various groups. The precise configuration of the resources, however, can be changed to the advantage of a particular group. That is, an issue can be expanded so as to ensure, or at least increase the likelihood of, its placement on the agenda.

The specific avenues for such expansion might include, but are not limited to, arousal, provocation, dissuasion, commitment, and affirmation (Cobb and Elder 1983, 142–50). The basic purpose behind the use of these avenues is to raise the level of consciousness among the public in an attempt to garner support for a cause. With the use of political symbols (such as conservatism, liberalism, capitalism, equality, etc.) through the mass media, both supporters and opponents of an issue seek to flex their political muscle on the political system. They either support or oppose the placement of an issue on the agenda, and behave accordingly.

In essence, what this amounts to is an expansion of the "scope of conflict" with reference to an issue (Schattschneider 1960, ch. 1-2). Incorporating more people in an issue conflict raises the importance of that issue and increases the likelihood of its placement on the agenda. Additionally, issues may also reach the agenda through diffusion (Walker 1969). That is, bureaucrats and public officials in the various states, for instance, communicate with each other, point out public policy problems, and suggest solutions that have been tried elsewhere.

The agenda, however, is subject to change. Shifts in agenda precipitate from a variety of sources. The political dynamics of issues frequently evolve over time, as key policymaking figures die, leave office, or simply move on. Changes in ideological balances or partisan majorities due to elections also bring about agenda changes (Brady 1982; Ginsberg 1976; Sinclair 1977). Moreover, public attitudes about issue stances often shift, thereby presenting policymakers with a new balance of political power. In addition, new institutions may be brought into the policymaking struggle. Possibly frustrated after losing a battle, one side of an issue might file a lawsuit, thereby bringing the court system into the process. Elsewhere, a group of interests might shift the struggle into another direction within the American federal system, moving the issue rivalry from state to federal institutions, or vice versa. For example, environmentalists have at times been exceptionally successful in winning mandated state and/or local approval of site placement for energy production plants and waste storage facilities.

All issues, however, must evolve through this process. Some reach the agenda faster than others, some receive more attention than others, and some are more favored than others, depending upon the circumstances.

Policy Formulation

Issues that have won placement on the policymaking agenda then enter the policy formulation stage. In the American political system, with the Founding Fathers' having designated Congress as the primary policymaking branch, public attention at this phase is normally directed toward winning legislative battles. At this stage, more than any other, the gamut of actors on the American political stage becomes involved, ranging from the president, through the courts, to interest groups, political parties, and constituencies.

The presidency and the executive branch normally play a key role at this stage. The president is at the center of influencing Congress in the legislative process. This happens both directly by convincing members of Congress and indirectly by convincing the public to pressure their representatives and senators (Kernell 2006). Presidents, however, can also make policies through certain executive means. For example, President Harry Truman, seeking to racially desegregate the armed services, did so by issuing an executive order as commander-in-chief of the military, rather than trying to win a bloody struggle anticipated in Congress. Or, more recently, President Barack Obama issued an executive order in 2014 to provide deportation relief to roughly five million undocumented immigrants.

No less important in the policymaking process is the role of the courts, the third branch of government under the constitutional separation of powers. Courts also become involved both directly and indirectly. Directly, civil rights advocates, for example, after losing struggles within numerous state and national institutions, won a major battle against racial segregation via the court system in the *Brown v. Board of Education of Topeka* decision in 1954. But more indirectly, courts are often called upon to interpret congressional statutes, and they do so through their power of judicial review. Therefore, courts also make policies, albeit frequently through interpreting legislative decrees.

Congress, of course, as indicated earlier, occupies center stage in the policymaking process. The ways in which Congress is involved, however, have changed over the years. All traditional models of policymaking in Congress place congressional committees at the center of that process. As Woodrow Wilson noted, "Congress in session is Congress on public exhibition, whilst Congress in its committee-rooms is Congress at work" (1901, 79). Recent research, however, has questioned the long-held notions about the centrality of congressional committees in the lawmaking process. At least on major pieces of legislation, Barbara Sinclair (2012) argues that nowadays Congress formulates policies on an ad-hoc basis. The contemporary lawmaking process in Congress does not fit the old how-a-bill-becomes-a-law diagram. Rather, bills bypass committees altogether or are referred to multiple committees. Decisions on the floors of the House and Senate are frequently made under complex rules and procedures. Nevertheless, regardless of the precise contours, Congress still occupies its constitutional and traditional centerstage.

In terms of policymaking, early observers of the modern Congress forwarded a tripartite structure of policymaking, one that included congressional committees, interest groups, and administrative agencies (Cater 1964, 17–22). This was commonly referred to as the "iron triangles," "cozy triangles," or "subgovernments." Each policy area, in other words, had its own iron triangle. Each of these units was intimately involved in the policymaking process and each worked to enhance and protect its own set of government programs. This was the model, the argument goes, prevalent in American policymaking in the 1950s.

Assessments of the lawmaking process of more recent years, which still place Congress in the middle, reveal a much more open and decentralized process than the iron triangles concept suggests. Hugh Heclo (1978) labels the policymaking process in terms of "issue networks." This model comprises large communities of individuals both inside and outside government, devoted both intellectually and emotionally, to a particular issue. These networks operate at all levels of government and include many individuals ranging from ordinary citizens to policy experts. Indeed, the fundamental requirement for entry into and involvement in an issue network is "watching, reading, talking about, and trying to act on particular policy problems" (Heclo 1978, 102). Issue networks, therefore, are akin to "advocacy coalitions," where advocates for a particular policy fight for a cause (Sabatier 1988).

Somewhat systematically, John Kingdon (1995) has outlined rather precise ways in which the legislative process comes to fruition. According to him, the agenda process works in three distinct streams: the problem (issues) stream, the policy (policies and alternatives) stream, and the political (political events) stream. When problems and solutions come together, or are coupled, a policy window opens. A policy window, therefore, opens and closes based upon the dynamics of the various streams and essentially represents a "window of opportunity" for the policymakers to pass legislation. In this process, as in issue networks or advocacy coalitions, a defining role is played by "policy entrepreneurs." These are policy advocates both inside and outside government who basically play the waiting game. They range from cabinet secretaries, to members of Congress, lobbyists, and bureaucrats. Their defining element is their willingness to fight for an issue. Most importantly, successful policy advocates are persistent. That is, successful entrepreneurs are ready and armed with solutions to problems and they wait for the right time. When that window opens, they strike and get bills passed.

Implementing Laws

Once policies are formulated, they are then implemented. Implementation simply is the process by which the just-formulated policies are put into practice (Mazmanian and Sabatier 1983). This stage of the policymaking process is as filled with strife as any in the life of an issue.

The implementation process, by definition, calls for change. Most policies are made to change existing ways of doing things. More so than any other, this stage of the policymaking process is continuous and evolutionary (Majone and Wildavsky 1978). A number of factors affect the implementation process. The implementation of programs "varies predictably with attributes of the policy, the implementors and their organizations, and the environment in which implementation decisions and actions take place" (Goggin et al. 1990, 20). Other factors, such as the technical difficulties involved, the diversity of the target group, the extent of behavioral change required, the attitudes and resources of the constituency groups, or the overall public support for or against a program, also affect implementation (Mazmanian and Sabatier 1983). All these factors can either help or hinder implementation.

What determines successful implementation of a program? In general, that depends upon the various inducements and constraints, or carrots and sticks. Specifically, Daniel Mazmanian and Paul Sabatier (1983) suggest a number of conditions for effective implementation. These include: (1) that the program be based upon sound theory, (2) that it be unambiguous, (3) that the implementors possess substantial managerial and political skill and be committed to the program, (4) that the program be actively supported by the constituencies and institutions involved in the implementation process, and (5) that the program receive priority at all times.

Moreover, Malcolm Goggin et al. (1990) emphasize the "communications" among the implementing actors as a key to successful implementation. Accordingly, the implementation of a program depends in part upon the content and the form of the message that the states and localities receive from the federal government and the reputations of the federal officials sending the messages. Content includes such things as the believability of the policy message and the resources that come with that message. Form includes the clarity as well as the consistency of a message with previous messages. Also, it helps tremendously if the federal officials communicating messages are perceived to have legitimacy and credibility within the political system. This suggests that the implementation process is top-down. In reality, however, the process is as much bottom-up as it is top-down. As such, subnational, in particular, local communities and interest groups, along with elected and appointed officials and agencies, can either induce or constrain the implementation of policies.

Arguably the prime actors at this stage are agencies and departments of the federal and state governments. Studies show that states are perhaps the most important players in the implementation of programs (Mazmanian and Sabatier 1983; Ripley and Franklin 1982; Ingram and Mann 1980). Indeed, according to these studies, implementation not only varies across states but it also varies across policies and over time. The agencies and departments implementing programs must have several things in mind. For example, officials implementing the policy must take great care to ensure that they understand exactly how the policymakers, such as the president or a majority of the members of Congress, intended for the policy to be implemented. At times, the wording of a law might be vague, as legislators forge compromises to assure passage of the program through the congressional labyrinth. Also, officials implementing policies must work to ensure that their efforts are coordinated successfully with other government (state, local, and/or federal) agencies, a task which sometimes can be quite daunting to members of any of the affected bureaucracies.

Hence, the implementation process is strongly dependent upon the personalities and goals of the people implementing the programs. Some refer to these individuals as "street-level bureaucrats" (Lipsky 1980). Depending upon their goals and personalities, they can either help or hinder the implementation of programs. What also contributes to their involvement, and indeed to the political nature of this process, is that they can be challenged by leaders at other levels of the federal system, or, either in public or through a lawsuit, by interest groups dissatisfied with how the policy is being implemented. Moreover, it is also quite common to see these bureaucrats become embroiled in fighting rival agencies over questions of jurisdiction, budget, and so forth.

In sum, the implementation stage can be lengthy and fraught with political peril for all concerned. It is in fact a policymaking stage as much as it is a policy implementation stage.

Policy Evaluation

The evaluation, or the policy redesign, process itself is a formal part of what has been termed the "feedback loop" of the policymaking process. Policy redesign is "the process by which an existing policy is modified, either by amending an existing statute or by adopting new rules and regulations, or by both amendment and rule change" (Goggin et al. 1990, 154). Here, essentially policymakers at the national level receive reactions to their new programs from throughout the political system. Ideally, this step is designed to formally analyze the relative success or failure of a policy. However, practically, it is the dissatisfaction with a new policy that comes into play more often than the satisfaction with a policy (Goggin et al. 1990, 39–40). The notes of dissatisfaction, or evaluation, can be heard from many quarters and are often the result of the different priorities that the various units of government have. For example, affected constituencies may intensely dislike the program, some element of the court system might rule the program to be unconstitutional, or another level of government might resist helping implement the program because of the unanticipated costs involved.

The most prominent players in the policy redesign process are the political agents and agencies found at the subnational levels of government. These agents include elected and appointed officials, such as governors, legislators, mayors, etc., at the state and local levels of governments. Affected constituencies, such as the individual voters or program providers, are also counted as agents. Agencies include various organizations, such as the state bureaucracy or a legislative committee, at the state and local level (Goggin et al. 1990, 160). The success of these agents and agencies in redesigning policies is generally dependent upon, but is not limited to, their credibility, the clarity and consistency with which they communicate their grievances to the national policymakers, and, of course, the willingness of the national policymakers to listen to those grievances and to redesign policies accordingly (Goggin et al. 1990, 161).

The "willingness to listen and to redesign" is generally dependent upon a variety of political factors, but most importantly upon the national policymaker's "world view" (Goggin et al. 1990, 162). So, for example, if a representative or a senator disagrees with a governor about the specific ways in which to redesign a policy or if he/she is ideologically opposed to the governor or if the redesigning might cost that representative or senator the next election, then the likelihood of that policy being modified is rather slim. National policymakers are unlikely to be responsive under these conditions.

Indeed, reactions actuated in this feedback process may become so intense that they reignite the agenda-setting process and the model repeats itself all over again. For example, after passing the Medicare Catastrophic Coverage Act in 1988, members of Congress repealed the measure the following year after intense negative reactions from many senior citizens who would have been called to finance part of the program. Although the feedback in that case took just a few months to affect the political system, in most cases the process takes years to come full circle.

IN THIS BOOK

This book provides case studies from which one may learn about how the American system works. Taken together, the scope of the case studies encompasses the entire policymaking process, exposing the interaction among all of the major power centers—interest groups, the media, courts, Congress, the president, and the federal bureaucracy, for example.

This book focuses on a broad array of major legislation passed by Congress since the turn of the twenty-first century—legislation that surrounds major issues/controversies facing the country. Each of the following seven policymaking chapters focuses on one program within a major policy area. Each chapter in one form or another covers the four phases identified above. Taken as a whole, this collection of case studies provides a picture of how the policymaking process works in the United States. For most issues, it is a continuing and often a messy saga. The list of noteworthy actors for each issue area can be long, complex, and ephemeral. Moreover, the breadth of the issues presented here illustrates the diversity of important issues that have been addressed, however successfully or ineptly, by the American policymaking system.

The rest of the book is as follows. In chapter 2, Michelle Wade analyzes the first major measure signed by President Obama, the Lilly Ledbetter Fair Pay Act. In chapter 3, Sean Foreman discusses the passage of the "Don't Ask, Don't Tell" Repeal Act. In chapter 4, Douglas Brattebo writes about the important and highly controversial passage of the Patient Protection and Affordable Care Act ("Obamacare") and the subsequent political wrangling. In chapter 5, Sunil Ahuja writes about the Higher Education Opportunity Act of 2008. In chapter 6, Peter Bergerson, Margaret Banyan, Ashley Skalecki, and Aleea Perry write about the highly politically charged Bipartisan Campaign Reform Act and the *Citizens United v. FEC* Supreme Court ruling. In chapter 7, Marcia Godwin, with Shandra McDonald, looks at the passage of the seminal Dodd-Frank Wall

Street Reform and Consumer Protection Act, which attempted to restore some of the regulation of the excesses of the nation's banking industry. In chapter 8, Kevin Buterbaugh chronicles the passage and evolution of the controversial USA PATRIOT Act. Finally, in chapter 9, we conclude by discussing some overarching themes of policymaking in a dynamic system.

NOTE

An earlier version of this chapter was published in *Government at Work: Issue Evolution, Passage, Implementation, and Feedback* (Kendall/Hunt, 1998, 2000), copyright by Sunil Ahuja and Robert Dewhirst.

REFERENCES

Baumgartner, Frank R., and Bryan D. Jones. 1993. *Agendas and Instability in American Politics*. Chicago: University of Chicago Press.
Brady, David. 1982. "Congressional Party Realignment and Transformations of Public Policy in Three Realignment Eras." *American Journal of Political Science* 26: 333–60.
Cater, Douglass. 1964. *Power in Washington*. New York: Vintage.
Cobb, Roger W., and Charles D. Elder. 1983. *Participation in American Politics: The Dynamics of Agenda-Building*, 2nd ed. Baltimore: Johns Hopkins University Press.
Easton, David. 1965. *A Framework for Political Analysis*. Englewood Cliffs, NJ: Prentice-Hall.
Ginsberg, Benjamin. 1976. "Elections and Public Policy." *American Political Science Review* 70:41-9.
Goggin, Malcolm L., Ann O'M. Bowman, James P. Lester, and Laurence J. O'Toole, Jr. 1990. *Implementation Theory and Practice: Toward a Third Generation*. New York: Harper-Collins.
Heclo, Hugh. 1978. "Issue Networks and the Executive Establishment." In *The New American Political System*, edited by Anthony King. Washington, D.C.: American Enterprise Institute.
Ingram, Helen, and Dean E. Mann, editors. 1980. *Why Policies Succeed or Fail*. Beverly Hills, CA: Sage.
Kernell, Samuel. 2006. *Going Public: New Strategies of Presidential Leadership*, 4th ed. Washington, D.C.: Congressional Quarterly.
Kingdon, John W. 1995. *Agendas, Alternatives, and Public Policies*, 2nd ed. New York: Harper-Collins.
Lipsky, Michael. 1980. *Street-Level Bureaucracy: Dilemmas of the Individual in Public Services*. New York: Russell Sage.
Majone, Giandomenico, and Aaron Wildavsky. 1978. "Implementation as Evolution." In *Policy Studies Review Annual*, edited by Howard Freeman. Beverly Hills, CA: Sage.
Mazmanian, Daniel A., and Paul A. Sabatier. 1983. *Implementation and Public Policy*. Glenview, IL: Scott, Foresman.
Ripley, Randall B., and Grace A. Franklin. 1982. *Bureaucracy and Policy Implementation*. Homewood, IL: Dorsey.
Sabatier, Paul A. 1988. "An Advocacy Coalition Framework of Policy Change and the Role of Policy-Oriented Learning Therein." *Policy Sciences* 21: 129–68.
Schattschneider, E.E. 1960. *The Semisovereign People: A Realist's View of Democracy in America*. New York: Holt, Rinehart, and Winston.

Sinclair, Barbara Deckard. 1977. "Party Realignment and the Transformation of the Political Agenda." *American Political Science Review* 71: 940–53.

Sinclair, Barbara. 2012. *Unorthodox Lawmaking: New Legislative Processes in the U.S. Congress*, 4th ed. Washington, D.C.: Congressional Quarterly.

Walker, Jack L. 1969. "The Diffusion of Innovation Among the American States." *American Political Science Review* 68: 880–99.

Wilson, Woodrow. 1901. *Congressional Government: A Study in American Politics*. Boston: Houghton, Mifflin.

TWO

Lilly Ledbetter Fair Pay Act (2009)

Michelle L. Wade

> "Equal pay for equal work is a fundamental American principle.
> We need leaders in this country who will fight for it.
> With all of us working together,
> we can have the change we need
> and the opportunity we deserve."
>
> —Lilly Ledbetter at the Democratic National Convention, 2008

On January 29, 2009, newly elected President Barack Obama signed the Lilly Ledbetter Fair Pay Act into law. This piece of legislation makes it easier for employees to sue employers for discrimination in pay. The law makes a discriminatory compensation decision illegal each time it occurs, as opposed to when the discriminatory decision is first made. The Lilly Ledbetter Fair Pay Act was passed in response to a 2007 Supreme Court decision that made it more difficult for employees to sue their employers for discriminatory pay. Lilly Ledbetter, the plaintiff in the case, had worked at Goodyear Tire Company in Gadsden, Alabama, for nineteen years and received considerably less pay than her male counterparts (Greenhouse 2007). Even though she was awarded damages of approximately $3.8 million in the U.S. District Courts, the Eleventh Circuit Court of Appeals reversed the decision, finding that Ledbetter's claim was time-barred. In other words, she had not filed the suit within the appropriate statute of limitations. In 2007, the Supreme Court reaffirmed the decision in the Court of Appeals. This Supreme Court ruling then provided the impetus for the Lilly Ledbetter Fair Pay Act. Justice Ruth Bader Ginsberg urged Congress to pass a law to correct what she perceived to be an injustice in this situation. Several members of Congress and interest groups then mobilized to introduce the new law. It was not until the turnover of the 2008 election, though, that there was enough political support to pass the bill.

This chapter includes an overview of gender wage gap, an overview of how gender stereotypes can impact employee evaluations, the story of Lilly Ledbetter's struggle for equal pay in the courts, and a description of the legislation that was created as a result of the 2007 Supreme Court decision in Ledbetter's case. Although long-term effects of the law are unknown, there is also a brief discussion of the impact that the law has had so far. This discussion addresses the number of complaints filed with the Equal Employment Opportunity Commission (EEOC) as well as recent court decisions post-Lilly Ledbetter Fair Pay Act.

PAY INEQUITY: WHY DO WOMEN EARN LESS THAN MEN?

Women earn less than men for a variety of reasons. Historically, they have not been paid the same wages even for the same jobs. Today, these inequities result because women are typically employed in lower paid professions and often work part-time. In addition, women do not have as much seniority as men because they tend to leave the workforce for a number of years due to childcare and parental responsibilities, which fall disproportionately on women (Conway, Ahern, and Steuernagel 1999). Thus, women are doing more unpaid labor in society, which, in turn, affects their paid labor. Liberal politicians and interest groups typically argue that the pay gap is a problem that the government needs to address, while conservative politicians and interest groups frequently take the position that women are not being intentionally discriminated against; it is their decisions to leave the workforce to care for children, etc. . . . so it is not the government's job to correct these problems since they are a result of individual choices. However, even when factors like leaving the workforce and working part-time are controlled for, there is still a portion of the wage gap that is unexplained. Wage disparity still persists between men and women occupying the same job in similar circumstances.

The discrimination that Lilly Ledbetter faced at Goodyear is not uncommon for women or for minorities.[1] In 2012, the Institute for Women's Policy Research reported that women's median salary was $37,791 as compared to men's median salary of $49,398. Expressed as a ratio, this means women's annual salaries were 76.5 percent of men's annual salaries—which means there is a gap of 23.5 percent. These figures were for full-time, year-round employees. The gap for weekly earnings as opposed to annual salaries was slightly better at 80.9 percent. Again, this measure is based in median earnings for full-time workers.

Although the wage gap between men and women has improved significantly over time, it has not improved since 2001. Previous decades saw far more improvement in the gender gap in pay. Table 2.1 from the Institute for Women's Policy Research maps the gender wage ratio from 1955–2012 for full-time workers. The table shows median annual earnings adjusted to 2012 dollars so that an adequate comparison can be made. There was negligible progress in the median annual earnings during the 1960s and 1970s. It was not until the 1980s that there was significant improvement. From 1981–1990, the wage gap was reduced by over ten percentage points. In the 1990s, it was further reduced by nearly four percentage points. From 2001–2010, the gap only improved a little more than one percentage point.

Given the current rate of improvement in regards to the gender pay gap, men and women will not receive equivalent earnings until 2058. Despite gains in educational levels, in the number of businesses owned by women, in the number of women in management, and in the number of professional jobs women occupy, women's wages have not kept pace with those of men.

GENDER STEREOTYPES AND PERCEPTIONS OF LEADERSHIP

Gender stereotypes often play a factor when it comes to the pay gap between men and women. Stereotypes by themselves are not necessarily problematic. After all, they serve a basic cognitive categorical function. Stereotypes refer to positive or negative beliefs about a group. For instance, a belief that women are more nurturing than men is a stereotype. This is a positive belief about women based on their group membership to the female sex. However, stereotypes become problematic if they are accompanied by prejudice or discrimination. Prejudice, or affect, refers to negative feelings about others based on their group membership. For instance, a negative feeling toward women in the workforce based on a belief that they belong in the home is prejudice. As it turns out, prejudice is a better predictor of discrimination than stereotypes (Fiske 1998). Discrimination, on the other hand, refers to the behavior that is directed at a person based on their group membership. Thus, not promoting a woman to a management position because of a negative belief that women are unsuitable for leadership positions would be discrimination.

Gender stereotypes are more accurately defined as sex-trait stereotypes (Williams and Best 1990). These stereotypes have four characteristics: they are cognitive, they are a set of beliefs, they refer to perceptions of what men and women are like, and they are perceptions shared by members of a specific group (Williams and Best 1990). All stereotypes are both descriptive and prescriptive. This means they not only describe how groups are viewed, they also prescribe how members of the group should behave (Deaux and LaFrance 1998).

Table 2.1. The Gender Wage Ratio and Real Earnings, 1955-2012

Year	*Women*	*Men*	*Female to Male Earnings Ratio*
1955	n/a	n/a	63.9
1960	22,094	36,414	60.7
1965	24,397	40,712	59.9
1970	28,084	47,305	59.4
1975	29,113	49,496	58.8
1980	29,701	49,370	60.2
1981	29,067	49,070	59.2
1982	29,726	48,143	61.7
1983	30,483	47,934	63.6
1984	31,105	48,863	63.7
1985	31,790	49,229	64.6
1986	32,439	50,473	64.3
1987	32,692	50,158	65.2
1988	32,831	49,706	66.1
1989	33,552	48,857	68.7
1990	33,752	47,128	71.6
1991	33,785	48,362	69.9
1992	34,267	48,411	70.8
1993	34,023	47,571	71.5
1994	34,013	47,261	72.0
1995	33,650	47,110	71.4
1996	34,545	46,833	73.8
1997	35,616	48,024	74.2
1998	36,375	49,713	73.2
1999	36,258	50,139	72.3
2000	36,610	49,661	73.7
2001	37,883	49,631	76.3
2002	38,542	50,315	76.6
2003	38,350	50,762	75.5
2004	37,968	49,582	76.6
2005	37,464	48,668	77.0
2006	37,021	48,119	76.9
2007	38,865	49,949	77.8

Year	Women	Men	Female to Male Earnings Ratio
2008	38,112	49,438	77.1
2009	38,828	50,440	77.0
2010	38,885	50,240	77.4
2011	37,886	49,200	77.0
2012	37,791	49,398	76.5

Note: These figures are based on median annual earning adjusted to 2012 dollars for full-time workers. Source: Institute for Women's Policy Research.

Thus, gender stereotypes are not benign; they shape how men and women behave. In fact, gender stereotypes tend to be more prescriptive than other kinds of stereotypes (Fiske 1998). For example, men and women who step out of prescribed gender roles or stereotypes might be "punished" for this transgression. Say a woman who is married and of childbearing age does not have children. She might be sanctioned socially for not ascribing to gender stereotypes that indicate women should have children. Even the reason why she does not have children becomes irrelevant. The woman may be seen as an "outcast" or "abnormal" even if the reason why she does not have children is beyond her control. Thus, women often feel pressured to have children because that is what is expected of them. According to social science researchers, the greater emphasis on the prescriptive dimension of stereotypes is due to a variety of factors including the experiences people share with those of the other gender (as opposed to other social groups where they are more isolated), the young age at which these prescriptions are learned, and the greater saliency of the category of gender (Fiske 1998).

Generally speaking, researchers have found that people tend to ascribe different characteristics to men and women. For instance, women are seen as more communal and men are seen as more agentic (Eagly 1987). Communal qualities include caring, affection, kindness, sympathy, helpfulness, emotionally expressive, selflessness, and sensitivity. Typical agentic qualities are assertiveness, aggressiveness, ambitiousness, independence, self-reliance, self-confidence, and a sense of adventure. Communal qualities, associated with women, have also been labeled as warmth and expressiveness or just expressiveness (Eagly 1987). Agentic qualities have also been labeled as instrumentality or competence and rationality (Eagly 1987). A well-known study by social psychology researchers uses a 300-item Adjective Check List to assess sex-stereotypes across twenty-five countries and find similar results across the countries they investigate (Williams and Best 1990). So, these stereotypes cross national boundaries and cultures.

The origin of gender stereotypes lays in the different social roles men and women occupy in society that stem from the division of labor between the sexes (Eagly 1987). In an empirical test of this theory, researchers found that people who were in domestic roles were perceived to be more communal, and people who were in paid employment were perceived to be more agentic. The division of labor between the sexes can lead to two different conditions. It can perpetuate gender-role expectations or sex-typed skills and beliefs, both of which lead to sex differences in behavior (Eagly 1987).

People bring these stereotypes to the workplace, and they influence perceptions of men and women in a number of aspects, including perceptions of male and female leadership, a chronic problem that Ledbetter reportedly faced during her tenure at Goodyear. Women in leadership positions who act in accordance with gender stereotypes are seen as "too soft" while women who act at odds with gender stereotypes are considered "too tough" (Catalyst 1997). The importance of gender stereotypes in evaluations of female managers is often dismissed because of the difficulty of proving their influence. Catalyst, an independent nonprofit organization, has performed numerous studies evaluating the impact of gender stereotypes on women's perceived performance in leadership positions. Although Catalyst researchers find substantial evidence of these trends, it is difficult to prove how factors such as gender stereotypes work to discriminate against individual women in the workplace since outcomes (e.g., promotions or the number of female managers) are all that can be observed. While there is evidence at the aggregate level in the scholarly literature, it is difficult to convince juries that women are being discriminated when it comes to compensation claims.

One way these stereotypes manifest themselves is through the low numbers of women in management positions. In 2012, women comprised 14.3 percent of executive officer positions in the top Fortune 500 companies and only 8.9 percent of the top earners in that category. In 2012, 27.1 percent of Fortune 500 companies had no women in executive positions (Catalyst 1997). These outcomes are usually dismissed as a pipeline problem, meaning that there are not enough women in the "pipeline" who have the appropriate qualifications. However, studies in a variety of fields show that men and women are evaluated differently when they apply for employment or promotion. Thus, gender stereotypes have very real consequences for women who are evaluated poorly or not promoted due to their gender.

LILLY LEDBETTER'S STORY

Lilly Ledbetter worked for Goodyear Tire Company in Gadsden, Alabama, from 1979-1998. During that time, she was trained to be a manager and was one of the first and few female managers in the plant. In fact, she was the only female manager to stay in the position for a substantial period of time. The other two women who had been promoted to management left the organization or returned to their previous job. Ledbetter contends that both of these women left management at Goodyear because of the hostile conditions they faced as women managers. The woman who returned to her previous job as a secretary reportedly did so because her promotion had not resulted in a corresponding pay increase. When Ledbetter first started at Goodyear, she made the same pay as all of the other male managers. However, Goodyear moved to a pay-for-performance system in 1981. This system allowed managers to be paid differently according to their performance levels, and the pay was confidential (United States House of Representatives, Committee on the Judiciary 2007). It was shortly after this that Ledbetter's salary began to diverge from that of her male counterparts.

Ledbetter reported being a victim of repeated hostile and discriminatory behavior during her tenure at Goodyear. In 1982, Ledbetter filed a sexual harassment complaint with the Equal Employment Opportunity Commission when one of her supervisors promised her good evaluations if she "met him" at a local hotel. Ledbetter complained to a manager about her supervisor's behavior, but nothing was done. It was at this point that Ledbetter turned to the EEOC. After her EEOC complaint, hostile treatment aimed at Ledbetter reportedly increased. In congressional hearing testimony, Ledbetter's prepared statement asserts that, "They tried to isolate me. People refused to talk to me. They left me out of important management meetings so I sometimes didn't know what was going on, which made it harder to do my job" (United States House of Representatives, Committee on the Judiciary 2007). After an investigation by the EEOC, Goodyear and the EEOC worked out a compromise where the individual who had allegedly sexually harassed her no longer supervised Ledbetter. In the U.S. District Court jury trial, Ledbetter's attorney presented evidence showing that Ledbetter's raises were higher before the complaint than afterwards (Ledbetter and Isom 2012).

One day before her shift in March of 1998, Ledbetter received an anonymous note in her mailbox (Ledbetter and Isom 2012). Listed on the note was her salary and those of her male counterparts. Ledbetter's salary was $44,724. Her highest paid male counterpart was making $59,028, but even the lowest paid male manager made more than Ledbetter. Shortly after receiving this anonymous tip in 1998, Ledbetter filed a complaint with the EEOC office in Birmingham, Alabama. Due to an early buyout option for retirement and personal circumstances, Ledbetter decided to retire later that same year. In 1999, the EEOC ruled that Ledbetter had the right to sue for the claim she had made against Goodyear in 1998.

Attorney Jon Goldfarb represented Ledbetter pro bono. The case was filed in 1999, and the trial was conducted in January of 2003. Ledbetter's initial claim fell under three different laws: the Equal Pay Act of 1963, Title VII of the Civil Rights Act of 1964, and the Age Discrimination in Employment Act of 1967. The Equal Pay Act of 1963 was an amendment to the Fair Labor Standards Act of 1938. It prohibits pay discrimination between women and men for equal work that requires similar skill, effort, and responsibility (Public Law 1963). Ledbetter argued that she was paid less than male managers at Goodyear despite the fact that the job required similar skill, effort, and responsibility. During the last part of her tenure at Goodyear, she was transferred to a technology engineer position, where she was again paid less than her male counterparts. Under the Equal Pay Act of 1963, Ledbetter could have sued two years from the date that she received her last discriminatory paycheck. In this case, Ledbetter could have foregone contacting the EEOC and waiting for notice of her right to sue. However, Ledbetter argued that she had faced far more than simply sex discrimination in wages.

Title VII of the Civil Rights Act covers a broader array of sex discrimination in employment practices, such as sexual harassment, promotions, and transfer decisions. As a result, Ledbetter's attorney sued under Title VII as well. Ledbetter argued that she had been excluded from management meetings, offered less overtime, rated harsher than her male counterparts, and transferred from her position as supervisor against her will, among a list of other discriminatory behaviors. Despite winning an award for outstanding performance in 1997, Ledbetter generally received unfavorable evaluations. Ledbetter's supervisors performed these evaluations, but Ledbetter never received any copies of her actual production numbers. Ledbetter had been asking for the numbers for years when she received poor evaluations, but none of her supervisors would provide her with them. Although Goodyear was able to provide documentation of Ledbetter's evaluations during the jury trial, the company was unable to provide any of Ledbetter's production numbers.

Ledbetter's third claim fell under the Age Discrimination in Employment Act of 1967. This act prohibits employment discrimination against individuals over the age of forty (Public Law 1967). When Ledbetter was transferred out of management, she was over the age of forty and was replaced by a younger, male co-worker. In fact, Ledbetter was the oldest manager at the time of the transfer.

The fourth claim of Ledbetter also fell under Title VII. Ledbetter filed a constructive discharge complaint, arguing she was essentially forced to quit her job due to a hostile work environment. After Ledbetter was transferred out of management, she became a technology engineer. It was in this position that she argued hostile work conditions forced her to quit.

As evidence, she pointed to medical treatment and depression while in this position.

Attempts to settle out of court failed, and the case was heard in the Federal District Court in Anniston, Alabama. Attorney Goldfarb was joined by his partner Mike Quinn in court. When Ledbetter was transferred out of management, her salary was $44,724. In the same year, her male counterparts earned the following: $55,679, $57,696, $58,226, $58,464, and $59,028 (Ledbetter and Isom 2012). The verdict in the case was mixed. The jury did not find Goodyear guilty of violating the Age Discrimination Act in Ledbetter's transfer from area manager to technology engineer. However, the jury did find Goodyear guilty of sex discrimination or retaliation in Ledbetter's transfer. And the jury did find in Ledbetter's favor on the claim of sex discrimination in salary. The jury awarded her $3.8 million in damages for back pay, damages on disparate salary claim, mental anguish, and punitive damages. Under Title VII, compensatory and punitive damages are capped according to a company's size, so the district judge reduced the $3.8 million award to $360,000.

Goodyear appealed the decision, arguing that Title VII requires discrimination complaints to be made within 180 days of the discriminatory action. Therefore, according to Goodyear, only Ledbetter's last salary review should have been under consideration (*Ledbetter v. Goodyear Tire Co., Inc.* 2007). The Eleventh Circuit U.S. Court of Appeals dismissed Ledbetter's complaint, ruling that there was no evidence of *initial* discrimination in the 180 days that could be reviewed for discriminatory practices. In essence, the court said Ledbetter should have filed her claim when she received her first discriminatory paycheck in the early 1980s. The Eleventh Circuit's decision was at odds with the decisions of some of the other Federal Court of Appeals. The precedent set in other courts is called the "paycheck accrual rule," which allowed wage-based discrimination claims to be filed as long as one paycheck occurred within the 180-day statute of limitations. Ledbetter's attorneys appealed the Eleventh Circuit Court's decision to the Supreme Court and asked Kevin Russell, an attorney based in Washington D.C., to take on the case.

At this point, several prominent interest groups wrote amici briefs requesting that the Supreme Court grant a writ of certiorari. Some of the groups that drafted a brief on Ledbetter's behalf were the National Partnership for Women and Families, the National Women's Law Center, the National Employment Lawyer's Association, and the American Civil Liberties Union (Cert Petition A). Among those who drafted an amicus brief on behalf of Goodyear, the respondent, were the Solicitor General (Cert Petition B), the U.S. Chamber of Commerce (Cert Petition C), and the counsel for Goodyear (Cert Petition D). These groups broke down largely along party lines, with liberal groups supporting Ledbetter and conservative groups supporting Goodyear.

PAY DISCRIMINATION AND THE COURTS

County of Washington v. Gunther

In 1981, the Supreme Court ruled in a 5–4 decision that cases involving unequal pay claim can be brought under Title VII of the Civil Rights Act of 1964 (Saltoun 1983). Title VII prohibits employment discrimination on the basis of race, color, religion, sex, and national origin. The rule established by the court in the case also said that the filing period for an EEOC claim begins with the discrete act of discrimination (*County of Washington, Oregon, et al. v. Gunther et al.* 1981). This becomes a sticking point in the *Ledbetter* case because the "discrete act" occurs without the explicit knowledge of the plaintiff.

National Railroad Passenger Corporation v. Morgan

In 2002, the Supreme Court issued a mixed verdict, ruling that Abner Morgan did not have the right to sue for damages of discrimination that had not occurred within the statute of limitations set by Title VII of the Civil Right Act. Thus, some of Morgan's claims were considered time barred and were dismissed. In the same ruling, however, the court said that some of the behavior outside of the statute of limitations was admissible if it contributed directly to a hostile work environment claim that occurred within the time frame (*National Railroad Passenger Corporation v. Abner Morgan* 2002). This also is relevant to the *Ledbetter* case because it does allow for certain factors to be taken into consideration outside of the statute of limitations.

Lilly Ledbetter v. Goodyear Tire and Rubber Co.

In *Lilly Ledbetter v. Goodyear Tire Company* (2007), the Supreme Court decided in a 5-4 decision that Ledbetter did not have the right to sue Goodyear under Title VII of the Civil Right Act of 1964 because she had not filed the claim within 180 days of the discriminatory pay decision. Even though discriminatory pay had occurred within the 180-day statute of limitations, the decision that resulted in disparate pay had not. Thus, Ledbetter was not entitled to a salary discrimination suit. Justices John Roberts, Antonin Scalia, Anthony Kennedy, Clarence Thomas, and Samuel Alito voted in the majority.

Justice Ruth Bader Ginsberg read her dissenting opinion from the bench, arguing that employees may not have knowledge of pay discrimination within 180 days (Greenwald 2010). Other justices who joined the dissent were John Paul Stevens, David Souter, and Stephen Breyer. In the dissent, Ginsberg (2007) writes:

> The Court's insistence on immediate contest overlooks common characteristics of pay discrimination. Pay disparities often occur, as they did in Ledbetter's case, in small increments; cause to suspect that discrimination is at work develops over time. Comparative pay information, moreover, is often hidden from employee's view. Employers may keep under wraps the pay differentials maintained among supervisors, no less the reasons for the differentials. Small initial discrepancies may not be seen as met for a federal case, particularly when the employee, trying to succeed in a nontraditional environment, is averse to making waves.

Ginsberg further argues that the majority's decision is a very narrow interpretation of Title VII and encourages Congress to correct this oversight.

The Supreme Court decision in *Ledbetter v. Goodyear* was a direct catalyst for the passage of the Lilly Ledbetter Fair Pay Act. The decision was handed down on May 29, 2007. Shortly after the decision, then-Senator Hillary Rodham Clinton announced that she would introduce a bill to correct this oversight upon the recommendation of Justice Ginsberg. Ultimately, Clinton was one of many cosponsors of the bill.

Not wasting any time, Congress took action on June 12, 2007, holding a hearing on the implications of the *Ledbetter* decision in the House Committee on Education and Labor. The committee was chaired by Representative George Miller (D-CA), the House sponsor of the Lilly Ledbetter Fair Pay Act, who opened the meeting with remarks about the importance of preventing pay discrimination. Representative Howard "Buck" McKeon, the ranking Republican on the committee, spoke in opposition to the bill:

> No one in this committee room agrees with gender discrimination. . . . At the same time, however, I hope no one in this room believes that we should put in place legislation that would keep employers indefinitely on the hook for employee claims of discrimination.
>
> Such legislation would be ripe for abuse, in my opinion, effectively allowing an employee to bring a claim against an employer decades after the alleged initial act of discrimination occurred. (United States House of Representatives, Committee on Education and Labor 2007)

Ledbetter testified at the hearing as well as Wade Henderson from the Leadership Conference on Civil Rights, Deborah Brake from the University of Pittsburgh School of Law, and Neal Mollen on behalf of the U.S. Chamber of Commerce. Henderson and Brake spoke in favor of proposing legislation to overturn the *Ledbetter* decision, while Mollen spoke against such a measure on that basis that employers would not be able to defend their positions without a reasonable statute of limitations.

On June 28, 2007, the House Subcommittee on the Constitution, Civil Rights, and Civil Liberties began hearings related to the impact of the *Ledbetter* decision on the enforcement of civil rights. Representative John

Nadler (D-NY), chair of the subcommittee, opened the hearing with concerns about the Supreme Court ruling: "I am very concerned once again that the Supreme Court has gone out of its way to read our anti-discrimination laws as narrowly as possible so as to deny relief to as many victims of discrimination as possible" (United States House of Representatives, Committee on the Judiciary 2007). Ledbetter testified before the committee at that hearing as well. Other witnesses included Martha Chamallas with the Moritz College of Law at Ohio State University, Neal Mollen with the U.S. Chamber of Commerce, and Marcia Greenberger with the National Women's Law Center (United States House of Representatives, Committee on the Judiciary 2007).

Ledbetter also testified before the Senate Judiciary Committee on September 23, 2008 (United States Senate A, Committee on the Judiciary 2008). Attorney Cyrus Mehri testified at the Senate committee hearing on Ledbetter's behalf in support of the Lilly Ledbetter Fair Pay Act (United States Senate B, Committee on the Judiciary 2008). Senator Patrick Leahy (D-VT), chairman of the committee, criticized the Supreme Court and the Federal Court of Appeal:

> The current Supreme Court seems increasingly willing to overturn juries who heard the factual evidence and decided the case. In employment discrimination cases, statistics show that the Federal Courts of Appeal are five times more likely to overturn an employee's favorable trial verdict against her employer than they are to overturn a verdict in favor of the corporation. That is a startling disparity for those of us who expect employees and employers to be treated fairly by the judges sitting on our appellate courts. (United States Senate B, Committee on the Judiciary 2008)

Testimony and remarks during both the Senate and House hearings indicate that Congress was clearly acting in direct response to the *Ledbetter* decision.

THE LILLY LEDBETTER FAIR PAY ACT OF 2009

The Lilly Ledbetter Fair Pay Act amended Title VII of the Civil Right Act of 1964 and the Age Discrimination in Employment Act of 1967, and it modified the Americans with Disabilities Act of 1990 and the Rehabilitation Act of 1973. The law makes any discriminatory compensation decision or practice illegal each time the act occurs. Thus, it overturns the Supreme Court's decision in *Ledbetter v. Goodyear Tire and Rubber Co.* that prevented Lilly Ledbetter from winning a discriminatory compensation claim because she had not filed suit within 180 days of the initial compensation decision that discriminated against her. In 2009, Rep. Miller sponsored the bill in the House of Representatives, and Senator Barbara Mikulski (D-MD) sponsored the bill in the Senate. There were 195 cosponsors in the House and fifty-four cosponsors in the Senate.

The bill was initially proposed in 2007, but failed to get the necessary votes in the Senate until after it was reintroduced in the wake of the 2008 election when Democrats increased their number of seats from 49 to 56. In 2007, the vote broke down largely along party lines, with Democrats supporting and Republicans opposing. On July 27, 2007, H.R. 2831 passed the House by a margin of 225 to 199 (Library of Congress A). In the Senate, Democrats did not have enough votes for cloture to end a Republican filibuster, so the legislation never came up for a vote (Library of Congress B). The 2008 election changed the party distribution in the Senate enough so that Democrats would have enough votes to end another potential GOP filibuster.

The Lilly Ledbetter Fair Pay Act was introduced again in the 111th Congress as H.R. 11 and S. 181 by Miller and Mikulski, respectively. In the House, H.R. 11 passed by a margin of 247–111 on January 9, 2009 (Library of Congress C). S. 181 passed the Senate with a 61–36 vote on January 22, 2009 (Library of Congress D). The Lilly Ledbetter Fair Pay Act was the first piece of legislation that President Obama signed into law on January 27, 2009. In his remarks, President Obama reinforced the message of equality in pay:

> So signing this bill today is to send a clear message that making our economy work means making sure it works for everybody. That there are no second-class citizens in our workplaces; and that it's not just unfair and illegal, it's bad for business to pay somebody less because of their gender or their age or their race or their ethnicity, religion, or disability; and that justice isn't about some abstract legal theory or footnote in a casebook. It's about how our laws affect the daily lives and the daily realities of the people; their ability to make a living and care their families and achieve their goals. (Obama 2009)

The Lilly Ledbetter Fair Pay Act makes reference to the Supreme Court case in Section 2 of the law, stating that the decision "undermines . . . statutory protections by unduly restricting the time period in which victims of discrimination can challenge and recover for discriminatory compensation decisions or other practices, contrary to the intent of Congress" and "ignores the reality of wage discrimination and is at odds with the robust application of the civil rights laws that Congress intended" (Public Law 2009). The law specifically states that it does not make any changes to current law in regards to pensions. Thus, businesses would not be held responsible for any losses of pensions due to a discriminatory wage decision. The legislation took effect on May 28, 2007, and applied to all claims under Title VII of the Civil Rights Act, the Age Discrimination in Employment Act, and the Americans with Disabilities Act that were "pending on or after that date" (Public Law 2009). The 180-day statute of limitations under Title VII was not changed, but the "act of discrimination" now applies to each time there is a discriminatory paycheck, not just when the initial decision is made. Implementation of the act still lies with the EEOC that monitors Title VII violations, and enforcement remains largely unchanged except for the designation of when the 180-day statute of limitations begins. See table 2.2 for a timeline of events in this case leading to the passage of the act.

THE CONSEQUENCES OF THE LILLY LEDBETTER FAIR PAY ACT

Critics of the law predicted that the Lilly Ledbetter Fair Pay Act would lead to a surge in pay discrimination cases. In general, these groups argued that it is unfair to sue businesses for wage discrimination that occurred far in the past. Further, critics argue that if employees are allowed to do this as a result of the act, then profit margins for businesses will suffer because they will need to retain employee records and documentation of pay decisions for a greater length of time. After the House passed the act, *Investor's Business Daily* warned: "There's no question that passage of the bill will do harm, with businesses being the primary casualty as lawsuit-happy trial attorneys will have an open field from which they can sue employers. It won't be long before companies begin racking up pay-discrimination suits they have no choice but to defend" (*Investor's Business Daily* 2009).

Although it is still probably too early to assess any long-term effects of the Act, the fears of critics have not come to fruition thus far. After the passage, there was not a surge of court cases claiming disparate pay (Greenwald 2010). It is true that some courts have reversed their previous decisions and have allowed cases to proceed, as in the case of *Mary Lou Mikula v. Allegheny County of Pennsylvania*, but that does not mean that the plaintiff will win, only that the case will be allowed to proceed (Greenwald 2010). There are several other cases like this that were allowed to proceed as a result of the Act, but these were not cases that were filed after the passage of the new law. In addition, as seen in figure 2.1, there does not appear to be a substantial increase in equal pay complaints under Title VII brought to the EEOC (U.S. EEOC).

The mean number of complaints that the EEOC received from Fiscal Year 1997 to 2012 was 1,049. The only years that show receipts greater than one standard deviation away from the mean are in 2000, 2001, and 2002. While claim receipts increased slightly in 2010, they were well within one standard deviation of the mean, and the number of complaints went back down in 2011. Thus, it does not appear that the EEOC is receiving a substantially higher number of complaints since the passage of the Lilly Ledbetter Fair Pay Act. This makes sense given that only the timeliness of the claim is affected by the law, not the merits of the case.

Table 2.2. Timeline of Events for the Lilly Ledbetter Fair Pay Act

March	1998	Lilly Ledbetter files complaint with EEOC
October	1999	EEOC issues Ledbetter right to sue letter
January	2003	Ledbetter awarded $3.8 million by jury in U.S. District Court
August	2005	Eleventh Circuit Court of Appeals reverses the District Court's ruling
		Court determines that Ledbetter's claim is time-barred by statute of limitations
November	2006	Supreme Court listens to oral arguments
May	2007	Supreme Court issues decision, upholding the Court of Appeals
		Justice Ginsberg reads dissent from bench, urging Congress to take action
June	2007	Representatives Steny Hoyer & George Miller announce a bill will be passed
		House Committee on Education and Labor holds a hearing to determine implications of *Ledbetter v. Goodyear*
		House Subcommittee on the Constitution, Civil Rights, and Civil Liberties holds a hearing: Impact of *Ledbetter v. Goodyear* on the Effective Enforcement of Civil Rights Laws
January	2008	Senate Committee on Health, Education, Labor & Pensions holds a hearing: The Fair Pay Restoration Act Ensuring Reasonable Rules in Pay Discrimination Cases
September	2008	Senate Committee on the Judiciary holds a hearing: Barriers to Justice: Examining Equal Pay for Equal Work
January	2009	House passes Lilly Ledbetter Fair Pay Act, 247–111
		Senate passes Lilly Ledbetter Fair Pay Act, 61–36
		President Obama signs Lilly Ledbetter Fair Pay Act into law

Source: Compiled by author.

Another possible explanation for this is that the law does not change the cap for damages that Title VII establishes, so plaintiffs would not potentially win greater damages even if discrimination were proven.

Further, an Institute of Management and Administration (IOMA) survey showed that only 19 percent of human resource employees reported that the Fair Pay Act has "affected their organization directly" (HR Focus 2010). The most common complaint revealed in the survey indicated that the Fair Pay Act has caused more of an administrative burden than anything else. Because the law does affect the timeliness of claims, businesses have an incentive to document and archive their pay practices in case

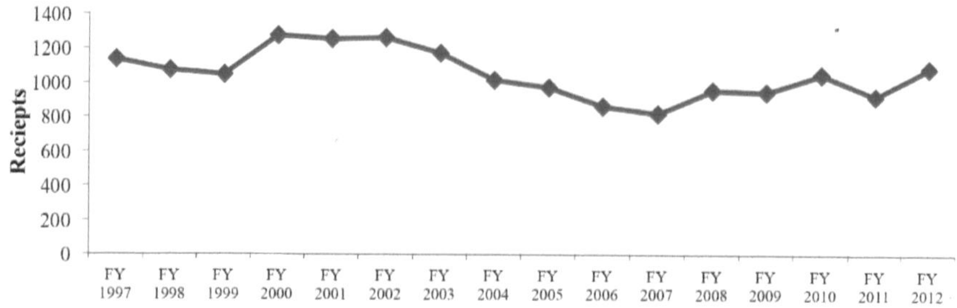

Figure 2.1. Equal Pay Act Charges (includes concurrent charges with Title VII, ADEA, and ADA) FY 1997–FY 2012. Source: United States Equal Employment Opportunity Commission, Equal Pay Act Charges, FY 1997–FY 2012.

they receive a claim that dates back further than they would normally keep in their administrative records.

In the courts, the interpretation of the Lilly Ledbetter Fair Pay Act appears to be mixed. Several courts have adopted a fairly narrow reading of the law, applying it only to compensation claims and not to promotions or job assignments, for example. Promotions and job assignments can certainly affect compensation, however, and some courts have interpreted the law more broadly. For example, in *Bush v. Orange County Corrections Department*, a district court of Florida allowed a plaintiff to sue based on the fact that not being promoted affected the plaintiff's compensation. Ultimately, the plaintiff lost the case when the court granted summary judgment requested by the employer. The court ruled that there was not enough evidence of prima facie discrimination (Baltodano and Martinez 2010). Courts have also ruled that the Lilly Ledbetter Fair Pay Act does not apply to other practices deemed illegal in Title VII if the claim has not been filed within 180 days of the act. For example, a district court in Mississippi ruled in *Johnson v. Watkins* that the act did not apply to a quid pro quo sexual harassment claim because it did not affect compensation (Baltodano and Martinez 2010).

The discovery rule may also affect the progress of discrimination claims. The discovery rule refers to the stage of legal proceedings in which evidence is obtained, either voluntarily or through subpoena. According to the discovery rule, a charge of discrimination should be filed promptly. In *Vuong v. New York Life Insurance Company*, the plaintiff lost because the complaint was filed in 2002 while the alleged discriminatory act (a promotion) occurred in 1998. In this case, the linkage between the discriminatory act and the disparate pay was not strong enough for a New York court to rule in the plaintiff's favor. However, in the same case the court allowed Vuong to challenge a performance-related bonus decision made in 1998. Clearly, it matters how the plaintiff frames the discriminatory act. In Louisiana, a district court came to a similar conclusion in *Olubadewo v. Xavier University*, ruling that the plaintiff had not taken prompt action when he knew of the discrimination. In this case, the plaintiff alleged that he had not been rehired at Xavier University based on race and national origin, but the court granted the employer's motion of summary judgment because the claim was not filed soon enough after the plaintiff's alleged discriminatory event occurred (Baltodano and Martinez 2010). In this case, it was considered a discrete event of which the plaintiff had knowledge.

CONCLUSION

The gender gap in wages is still a significant problem in the United States even after the passage of the Equal Pay Act of 1963 and the Civil Rights Act of 1964. Although women made large gains in wages during the 1980s and 1990s, the gap has remained largely stagnant since 2001. Unfortunately, sex stereotypes disadvantage women in the workplace, but it is difficult to convince juries of sex discrimination, particularly when there are pay-for-performance systems in place. Ledbetter did receive lower evaluations than most of her male counterparts; however, Goodyear never provided her or the court with her actual production numbers—just the supervisor evaluations. As evidenced by Ledbetter's situation, it is often difficult to prove sex discrimination in employment decisions. Although Ledbetter won in the Federal District Court, the decision was overturned in the Eleventh Circuit Court of Appeals. The U.S. Supreme Court in *Ledbetter v. Goodyear* upheld the Court of Appeals' decision. Ultimately, the Supreme Court took a narrow interpretation of Title VII by saying that Ledbetter should have sued when her pay first started to diverge from those of her male colleagues even though salary information was confidential. The Court ruled that Ledbetter's claim was time-barred since she had not filed suit soon enough.

In the case of the Lilly Ledbetter Fair Pay Act, the impetus for the legislation was the Supreme Court's narrow ruling in *Ledbetter v. Goodyear*. Justice Ginsberg played a pivotal role in her dissenting opinion by encouraging Congress to take action to correct the Court's ruling. Liberal groups mobilized in opposition to the ruling, and the 2008 election played a significant role in the passage of the law. Senate Democrats did not have enough support in the Senate to gain passage until after the election. Only time will tell what impact the Lilly Ledbetter Fair Pay Act will have on litigation in employment discrimination cases, but so far the effects seem relatively small. While it is true that employers will need to document all promotion and compensation decisions, many businesses were already doing this. There does not appear to be a surge in Title VII complaints of sex discrimination pay claims with the EEOC, and businesses themselves report the primary effect of an added administrative burden, not an increase in lawsuits.

NOTE

1. Although this chapter focuses primarily on the pay gap between women and men, there is significant pay discrimination on the bases of race and ethnicity as well. Even though the Lilly Ledbetter Fair Pay Act was initiated due to a sex discrimination claim, it is applicable to other forms of discrimination as set forth in Title VII, the Age Discrimination Act, and the Americans with Disabilities Act.

REFERENCES

Baltodano, Hernaldo J., and David Martinez. 2010. "Determining the Reach of the Lilly Ledbetter Fair Pay Act." *Los Angeles Lawyer*. Los Angeles County Bar Association.

Cert Petition A, *Ledbetter v. Goodyear*, No. 05-1074, Brief of the National Partnership for Women and Families et al. as Amici Curiae in Support of the Petitioner, www.aclu.org/womens-rights/aclu-amicus-brief-ledbetter-v-goodyear-tire-rubber-co.

Cert Petition B, *Ledbetter v. Goodyear*, No. 05-1074, Brief for the United States as Amici Curiae Supporting Respondent.

Cert Petition C, *Ledbetter v. Goodyear*, No. 05-1074, Brief of the Chamber of Commerce of the United States of America and the National Federal of Independent Business Legal Foundation as Amici Curiae in Support of Respondent, supreme.lp.findlaw.com/ supremecourt/briefs/05-1074/05-1074.mer.ami.commerce.pdf.

Cert Petition D, *Ledbetter v. Goodyear*, No. 05-1074, On Writ of Certiorari to the United States Court of Appeals for the Eleventh Circuit, Brief for the Respondent, www.oyez.org/sites/default/files/cases/20002009/2006/2006051074/briefs/respondent/Brief%20for%20Respondent%20Goodyear%20Tire%20and%20Rubber%20Company,%20Inc.pdf.

Conway, Margaret M., David W. Ahern, and Gertrude A. Steuernagel. 1999. *Women and Public Policy: A Revolution in Progress*. Washington, D.C.: Congressional Quarterly.

County of Washington, Oregon, et al. v. Gunther et al. No. 80-429. Supreme Court of the United States. Argued March 23, 1981. Decided June 8, 1981.

Deaux, Kay, and Marianne LaFrance. 1998. "Gender." In *The Handbook of Social Psychology*, 4th ed., Vol. I, edited by Daniel T. Gilbert, Susan T. Fiske, and Gardner Lindzey. New York: McGraw-Hill.

Eagly, Alice H. 1987. *Sex Differences in Social Behavior: A Social-Role Interpretation*. New Jersey: Lawrence Erlbaum.

Fiske, Susan T. 1998. "Stereotyping, Prejudice, and Discrimination." In *The Handbook of Social Psychology*, 4th ed., Vol. I, edited by Daniel T. Gilbert, Susan T. Fiske, and Gardner Lindzey. New York: McGraw-Hill.

Ginsberg Dissent, 550 U.S. 2007, *Lilly Ledbetter v. Goodyear*, No. 05-1074. Supreme Court of the United States, May 29, 2007.

Greenhouse, Linda. 2007. "Justices' Ruling Limits Lawsuits on Pay Disparity." *New York Times*, May 30.

Greenwald, Judy. 2010. "Ledbetter Fair Pay Law Hasn't Flooded Courts." *Business Insurance*, February 8.

Ledbetter v. Goodyear Tire Co., Inc. No. 05-1074. Supreme Court of the United States. Argued November 27, 2006. Decided May 29, 2007.

Ledbetter, Lilly, with Lanier Scott Isom. 2012. *Grace and Grit: My Fight for Equal Pay and Fairness at Goodyear and Beyond*. New York: Crown Archetype.

Library of Congress A, Congressional Record, 110th Congress. 2007. thomas.loc.gov/cgi-bin/query/D?r110:26:./temp/~r110Q5oC3I.
Library of Congress B, Congressional Record, 110th Congress, 2007. thomas.loc.gov/cgi-bin/query/D?r110:11:./temp/~r110Q5oC3I.
Library of Congress C, Congressional Record, 111th Congress, 2009. thomas.loc.gov/cgi-bin/query/D?r111:51:./temp/~r111l9zSU8.
Library of Congress D, Congressional Record, 111th Congress, 2009. thomas.loc.gov/cgi-bin/query/D?r111:59:./temp/~r111l9zSU8.
National Railroad Passenger Corporation v. Abner Morgan. No. 00-1614. Supreme Court of the United States. Argued January 9, 2002. Decided June 10, 2002.
Obama, Barack. 2009. Remarks on Signing the Lilly Ledbetter Fair Pay Act of 2009. Daily Compilation of Presidential Documents, January 29.
Public Law 88-38, Equal Pay Act of 1963, June 10, 1963.
Public Law 90-202, Age Discrimination in Employment Act, December 15, 1967.
Public Law 111-2, "Lilly Ledbetter Fair Pay Act of 2009," 111th Congress, January 29, 2009.
Saltoun, Jule. 1983. "County of Washington v. Gunther: Sex-Based Discrimination Extends beyond the Equal Pay Act." *Loyola of Los Angeles Law Review* 16 (1): 151.
"Saying No To Lilly." 2009. *Investor's Business Daily*, editorial, January 23.
"The Double-Bind Dilemma for Women in Leadership." 1997. Catalyst.
United States House of Representatives, Committee on the Judiciary, Subcommittee on the Constitution, Civil Rights, and Civil Liberties, June 28, 2007.
United States House of Representatives, Committee on Education and Labor, Hearing on Justice Denied? The Implications of the Supreme Court's Ledbetter V. Goodyear Employment Discrimination Decision, June 12, 2007.
United States Senate A, Committee on the Judiciary, Hearing on Barriers to Justice: Examining Equal Pay for Equal Work, Testimony of Lilly Ledbetter, September 23, 2008.
United States Senate B, Committee on the Judiciary, Hearing on Barriers to Justice: Examining Equal Pay for Equal Work, Testimony of Cyrus Mehri, September 23, 2008.
United States Equal Employment Opportunity Commission, Equal Pay Act Charges, FY 1997–FY 2012.
"What Has Changed Since Enactment of Lilly Ledbetter?" 2010. HR Focus, Bureau of National Affairs.
Williams, John E., and Deborah L. Best. 1990. *Measuring Sex Stereotypes: A Multination Study*. Newbury Park: Sage.

THREE

The Struggle to Repeal Don't Ask, Don't Tell (2010)

Sean D. Foreman

The path to ending legal discrimination against homosexuals in the military was a long and arduous road. It formally ended when the U.S. Senate voted on December 18, 2010, in a lame duck session, to pass legislation advanced in the U.S. House of Representatives that ended the ban on openly gay service members. President Obama signed the repeal bill into law in December 2010 during a lame duck session of the 111th Congress. The repeal was effective in September 2011.

Section 654 of Title 10 of the United State Code, a law more commonly called Don't Ask, Don't Tell, was enacted as a political compromise policy in 1993. The issue was placed on the public policy agenda during the 1992 campaign as Democratic presidential candidate Bill Clinton discussed ending discrimination against gays in the military as a policy issue. Upon taking office, there was pressure from liberal groups to follow through but still significant opposition from Congress. This lead to the middle position that would attempt to ban discrimination by keeping the sexual orientation of service members in the closet and include the intent to limit the pursuance of cases concerning the sexuality of members of the armed forces. If you could not ask about someone's sexual orientation, and they did not have to tell any personal information, then there was not technically discrimination against gays in the U.S. military.

HOW DON'T ASK, DON'T TELL BECAME AN ISSUE

The policy known as Don't Ask, Don't Tell (DADT) started with an executive order announced by President Clinton on January 29, 1993. It ended with President Obama signing a law to eliminate the policy in 2010. The path to get to that point travelled through several legislative sessions and the executive decisions from the desks of several presidents.

In 1950, President Harry S. Truman signed the Uniform Code of Military Justice. That law set up discharge rules for homosexual service members. This was a codification of the *de facto* policy of the military to date. Truman had issued an executive order to desegregate the military in 1948, a decision that helped advance the civil rights movement and to the ultimate end of legal discrimination based on race. Homosexuality was considered a dangerous category of behavior along with anarchists and communists included on a list of people deemed subversive or un-American by the U.S. State Department in 1950. There were 4,380 people discharged from the military for homosexuality between 1947 and 1950 (Adam 1995; Shilts 2005).

President Jimmy Carter initiated a movement to a tighter policy in the 1970s. In 1982, President Ronald Reagan's Department of Defense (DOD) formalized the policy and issued a directive declaring that "homosexuality is incompatible with military service. The presence in the military environment of persons who engage in homosexual conduct or who, by their statements, demonstrate a propensity to engage in homosexual conduct, seriously impairs the accomplishment of the military mission" (GAO Report 1992). Servicemen or women who engaged in homosexual acts or even stated that they were homosexual or bisexual were discharged.

The DOD defined homosexual as "a person, regardless of sex, who engaged in, desires to engage in, or intends to engage in homosexual acts." Such acts were defined as "bodily contact, actively undertaken or passively permitted, between members of the same sex for the purpose of satisfying sexual desires" (GAO Report 1992).[1] According to a General Accounting Office report issued in 1992, DOD expelled 1,500 men and women annually on average between 1980 and 1990 with a high of around 2,000 in 1982 and a low of around 1,000 in 1990. About 78 percent were men and most were white.

The 1992 GAO report was issued in response to a request by Congressmen John Conyers, Jr. (D-MI), Gerry E. Studds (D-MA), and Ted Weiss (D-NY) to review the anti-homosexual policy. These members introduced a bill on May 19, 1992, to prohibit discrimination in the military on the basis of sexual orientation. The GAO report did not make a recommendation or take a position on the proposal that ultimately did not advance. In 1989, Rep. Studds released a previously suppressed Pentagon report that stated that sexuality was unrelated to job performance and started to get the idea on the policy agenda (Cave 2006).

During the 1992 presidential campaign, the main candidates for the Democratic Party each stated that they supported ending the ban on gays openly serving in the military. Arkansas Governor and Democratic nominee Bill Clinton made a campaign promise to lift the ban on homosexuals in the military if elected. After his inauguration, Clinton said in a news conference on January 29, 1993, "The issue is not whether there should be homosexuals in the military. Everyone concedes that there are. The issue is whether men and women, who can and have served with real distinction, should be excluded from military service solely on the basis of their status. And I believe they should not" (Clinton 1993). Clinton called for Secretary of Defense Les Aspin to submit a draft executive order for implementation by July 15 upon consulting with military and congressional leaders as well as concerned citizens.

But the Clinton Administration's efforts met resistance from conservative Democrats in Congress, especially Senator Sam Nunn (D-GA), who was chairman of the Senate Armed Services Committee. This compromise was initially referred to as the "don't ask, don't tell, and don't pursue" policy although Clinton did not use the "don't pursue" line in public speeches. The "don't pursue" provision was akin to "don't investigate," which was an ultimate goal of homosexual rights groups. The "don't ask, don't tell" language that was ultimately popularized was used by Sen. Nunn (Burrelli and Feder 2009).

Don't Ask, Don't Tell came out of a compromise between Congress and President Clinton. Congressional leaders inserted language in a bill that required the military to abide by the directive introduced by Reagan. In December 1993, Clinton issued a directive that stated that military recruiters were forbidden from asking prospective enlistees about their sexual orientation and commanders were not permitted to pursue investigations of suspected homosexuals or homosexual behavior without compelling evidence.

Over the next seventeen years under DADT, the number of military personnel discharged for homosexuality increased (see table 3.1). There were 617 discharges in 1994 and then 997 in 1997 to a high of 1,227 in 2001 (Weiner 1998). Gay rights advocates claimed that this was due to increased incidences of gay members being outed by commanders. Pentagon officials, including Clinton's second term Secretary of Defense William Cohen, claimed the increased numbers were due to more voluntary declarations of homosexuality as a means of getting out of the military for those who decided they wanted to leave. Pentagon spokesman Kenneth Bacon said, "We think the rise is almost exclusively explained by the increase in the numbers of people stating they are homosexuals. We think they are voluntary statements. We can only speculate as to why they are doing this" (Weiner 1998). Voluntary declarations were forbid-

Table 3.1. Total Number of DADT Discharges During Fiscal Year, 1994-2009

Year	Total Number of Homosexual Discharges	Percentage of Total Active Armed Forces
1980	1,754	0.086
1981	1,817	0.088
1982	1,998	0.095
1983	1,815	0.085
1984	1,822	0.085
1985	1,660	0.077
1986	1,643	0.076
1987	1,380	0.063
1988	1,101	0.051
1989	996	0.047
1990	941	0.046
1991	949	0.048
1992	730	0.040
1993	682	0.040
1994	617	0.038
1995	757	0.050
1996	858	0.058
1997	997	0.069
1998	1,145	0.081
1999	1,034	0.075
2000	1,212	0.088
2001	1,227	0.089
2002	885	0.063
2003	770	0.054
2004	653	0.046
2005	726	0.052
2006	612	0.044
2007	635	0.046
2008	634	0.045
2009	428	0.026
2010	261	0.015

Source: *Congressional Research Service* 2009; Keori 2011; author research.

den under the order. Gay rights advocates disputed this explanation for the increase.

Some groups claimed that even under DADT many personnel felt harassment from commanders and that many commanders seemingly did not understand the policy. A former Army captain who was co-director of the Servicemembers Legal Defense Network noted that there was little training on the policy or rules related to it. This allowed commanders to interpret the rules to their favor.

A member could also be discharged if there was evidence that they had engaged in or attempted to engage in a homosexual act. A homosexual act was defined quite broadly to the point that it could include hugging and hand-holding (GI Hotline 2011). If a member stated that they were homosexual or bisexual, or if they attempted to marry someone of the same sex in a state where it was permitted, this would also lead to discharge.

The total number of service members discharged under DADT is difficult to determine and varies by source. Discharged personnel would have to report to one of several advocacy groups that kept track of this statistic. An estimate by the GI Rights Hotline is that more than 14,500 military personnel members were discharged for homosexual orientation during the DADT period (GI Hotline 2011). Numbers gathered from Servicemembers Legal Defense Network and other sources has the number at 13,650. From 1997 to 2001, there were more than 1,000 members per year discharged. The numbers steadily decreased each year thereafter, reaching lows of 428 in 2009 and 261 in 2010. Not all of the discharges were involuntary. Some reported that they sought discharge because they felt threatened based on their sexual orientation.

DADT reached the federal courts through the issue of military recruiters on college campuses. The Supreme Court ruled unanimously in 2006 that the federal government could withhold funding to force universities to accept military recruiters that acted in violation of university nondiscrimination policies. The law was upheld in federal courts five times.

Another issue was separation pay for those who were involuntarily discharged. Under the Defense Department policy, many of those discharged due to DADT were subject to having their separation pay cut in half. A class action suit in *Collins v. United States* was brought forth in 2010 by the American Civil Liberties Union and its New Mexico affiliate. The lead plaintiff, Richard Collins, was honorably discharged after he was observed kissing another man. A settlement announced in January 2013 provided coverage for service personnel who were discharged on or after November 19, 2004, the furthest back it could be given due to the statute of limitations. The total pay owed to those service members was about $2.4 million. Service members were entitled to separation pay if they were involuntarily and honorably discharged after completing at least six years of service (Ring 2013).

In the campaign to replace Clinton, George W. Bush said "I'm a 'don't ask, don't tell' man" during the 2000 New Hampshire presidential primary debate. After the election, Bush appointed Colin Powell to be Secretary of State, who had supported DADT as an Army General when it was established, and while presiding over military conflicts in Afghanistan and Iraq, Bush did not discuss any reforms to DADT.

In 2003, during Bush's first term, former president Clinton publicly called for an end to "don't ask, don't tell," and the repeal effort slowly started climbing on the national policy agenda.

The momentum to repeal DADT gained steam during the 2008 presidential nomination campaign. Several Democratic candidates raised their hand when asked during a debate in June 2007 on CNN if they would support eliminating DADT, including top candidates Hillary Clinton, John Edwards, and Barack Obama. After the election, repeal of DADT became a stated policy priority for President Obama but not a pressing one given the economic challenges the country faced and the military's involvement in two wars when he took office.

The House voted 234–194 in May 2010 to approve an amendment to the National Defense Authorization Act (NDAA), the annual defense spending bill, which would end the ban on homosexuals in the military. There was also a provision, however, that the ban would not end until the Pentagon conducted a study on how the change would impact the armed forces. An identical provision passed the Senate Armed Services Committee but failed to pass the full Senate.

Work on the Pentagon report started in March and was released on November 30. The study of military service members concluded that openly gay troops posed a low risk to the armed forces' abilities and effectiveness. By then, top military officials were on the record in support of repealing the policy. During testimony to the Senate Armed Services Committee in February 2010 regarding DADT, then Secretary of Defense Robert Gates said, "I fully support the president's decision. The question before us is not whether the military prepares to make this change but how we must—how we best prepare for it" (Whitlock and Jaffe 2010).

Admiral Mike Mullen, Chairman of the Joint Chiefs of Staff under Obama, added his own endorsement saying his "personal belief that allowing gays and lesbians to serve openly would be the right thing to do. No matter how I look at this issue, I cannot escape being troubled by the fact that we have in place a policy which forces young men and women to lie about who they are in order to defend their fellow citizens. For me personally, it comes down to integrity - theirs as individuals and ours as an institution. I also believe that the great young men and women of our military can and would accommodate such a change. I never underestimate their ability to adapt."

General Powell, a former Joint Chiefs chairman, also said his views on the policy had evolved. "In the almost 17 years since the 'Don't Ask,

Don't Tell' legislation was passed, attitudes and circumstances have changed. I fully support the new approach presented to the Senate Armed Services Committee by Secretary Gates and Admiral Mullen" (Baker 2010).

Another former Chairman of the Joint Chiefs of Staff, General John Shalikashvili, testified that, "Tradition is a critical military value, and the armed forces have a long-standing tradition of banning gay men and lesbians. Equally important military traditions, however, are learning and adapting—and my colleagues made claims as if no new knowledge has been acquired over past decades, during which time Israel and Britain joined more than twenty other nations to allow openly gay individuals to serve without overall problems" (Shalikashvili 2009).

A letter signed by 104 retired generals and admirals stated, "As is the case with Great Britain, Israel and other nations that allow gays and lesbians to serve openly, our service members are professionals who are able to work together effectively despite differences in race, gender, religion and sexuality. Such collaboration reflects the strength and the best traditions of our democracy" (Generals and Admirals Request 2008). This was an increase from a similar statement that was signed by twenty-eight former generals and admirals the previous year (Fox 2008).

Despite this show of strength by former military leaders, the repeal efforts stalled in the Senate. In the summer of 2010, as Democrats held fifty-seven seats, and with two independents that caucused with Democrats, they fell just short of the sixty votes needed to break a Republican filibuster. Republicans were able to use this as leverage in negotiations over ending the Bush-era tax cuts that were set to expire at the end of the 2010 calendar year.

On December 9, Senate Republicans filibustered a vote on repealing DADT as part of the defense reauthorization bill. Senator Joe Lieberman (I-CT), a former Democrat turned Independent and a moderate in the middle of the Senate ideological stream, worked to build Senate support for the repeal bill. Lieberman found bipartisan support from other moderate senators like Susan Collins (R-ME) and Mark Udall (D-CO).

The House passed a standalone bill to repeal DADT a by 250-175 vote on December 15. This provided optimism for advocates to get Senate support in the lame duck session. On December 18, 2010, the repeal passed the Senate by a 65–31 vote. President Obama signed it into law on December 22, signaling an end to the seventeen-year legal ban on gays openly serving in the military. "This is the civil rights issue of this generation, and equality is not up for discussion. The notion that all men and women are created equal is an American value, and that is why I am so proud to finally see the discriminatory Don't Ask Don't Tell policy repealed," said House Minority Leader Steny Hoyer (D-MD) (HRC nd).

INSTITUTIONAL AND POLITICAL ACTORS

Congress

The original DADT compromise was born out of resistance in Congress to President Clinton's overtures to end the ban on gays serving openly in the military. Sen. Nunn and other conservative Democrats, along with Republicans and strong support from military leaders, were able to implement the policy and keep it in place for seventeen years.

Support for repealing DADT was relatively strong among liberal Democrats in the House starting in 2005. By contrast, House Republicans and Blue Dog Democrats, some of whom were elected in 2006 when Democrats regained majority control, were resilient in their opposition. Repeal amendments introduced did not gain enough support to get voted out of committee until 2010 when the repeal bill ultimately passed the House with support from Democrats and moderate Republicans in a lame duck Congress.

Congressman Marty Meehan (D-MA) first introduced a Military Readiness Enhancement Act in 2005 (National, nd). The bill had 122 cosponsors and would have prohibited discrimination based on sexual orientation against any member of the armed forces or anyone seeking to become a member. The bill was referred to the House Subcommittee on Military Personnel and no major action was taken (Military 2005). The bill was introduced again in 2007 and stalled in committee. Representative Ellen Tauscher (D-CA), with 192 cosponsors, introduced a similar bill in March 2009. Again, it did not get voted out of the subcommittee.

After the retirements of Meehan and Tauscher, Congressman Patrick Murphy (D-PA), an Iraq war veteran, took up the cause and was a leader in getting the repeal passed in the House. Murphy was the first veteran from the 2003 Iraq war to be elected to Congress, winning a narrow race against incumbent Mike Fitzpatrick during the 2006 Democratic wave election. After being reelected in 2008, Murphy was then defeated in 2010 by Fitzpatrick, who was aided by the Tea Party surge. Murphy, a member of the Blue Dog Democratic caucus, worked to convince other moderate Democrats to support this politically risky bill while himself serving as a lame duck.

Republicans, bolstered by the Tea Party movement, gave Democrats a "shellacking" (the word used by President Obama) in November 2010 and won majority control of the House (but not the Senate). This increased calls for Congress to act during the lame duck session to end DADT before the new, more conservative House would be sworn-in in January 2011.

Sen. Lieberman was a key Senate dealmaker on ending DADT. The former Democrat-turned-Independent from Connecticut served as a bipartisan bridge in the upper chamber. Lieberman was the Democratic nominee for vice president in 2000 but then lost his Democratic primary in 2004 due to supporting the Bush policy for the war in Iraq and other hawkish foreign policy positions. Lieberman won reelection to the Senate as an Independent and caucused with the Democrats.[2] He worked on finding the sixty votes needed to bring cloture to debate on repealing DADT.

Senator John McCain (R-AZ), the 2008 Republican nominee for president, was a vocal opponent of the repeal. McCain combated the comments by Admiral Mullen and the individual branch Chiefs of Staff. He favored the view of the Marine Commandant who was heartily opposed to the repeal and took issue with the Working Group's study results, though McCain actually stated differing positions on the policy over the years (Volsky 2010).

Senators Olympia Snowe (R-ME) and Susan Collins (R-ME), moderate Republicans from Maine, Scott Brown (D-MA), Lisa Murkowski (R-AK), John Ensign (R-NV), Richard Burr (R-NC), Mark Kirk (R-IL), and George Voinovich (R-OH) crossed party lines in the Senate to support the repeal. All Democrats voted for the repeal except Senator Joe Manchin (D-WV), a conservative Democrat who did not vote. Three Republicans, Senators Orrin Hatch (R-UT), Judd Gregg (R-NH), and Jim Bunning (R-KY) did not vote on the final Senate repeal bill.

Presidential Leadership and Actions

Secretary of Defense Bob Gates ordered the review on March 2, 2010, and appointed Jeh Charles Johnson, General Counsel of the Department of Defense, and General Carter F. Ham, U.S. Army, to co-chair the committee. A team of forty-nine military and nineteen civilian personnel from across the defense and military services aided the study. The two main goals of the review were: (1) to "assess the impact of repeal of Don't Ask, Don't Tell on military readiness, military effectiveness, unit cohesion, recruiting, retention, and family readiness; and (2) to recommend appropriate changes, if necessary, to existing regulations, policies, and guidance in the event of repeal" (Report 2010, 1). They were also charged with developing a plan of action to support implementation of a repeal policy. The report claimed that this was likely the largest and most comprehensive personnel policy related study in the history of the military.

The Department of Defense released a 256-page report on a comprehensive study of the issues associated with the repeal. The report was the result of a nine-month study of the issue. The Working Group collected 115,052 survey responses from service members and from 44,266 military spouses. There were ninety-five informational forums conducted with more than 24,000 service members and 140 smaller focus group sessions with about 14,000 service members. They also received 72,384 online entries. There were confidential communications with 2,691 service members, of which 296 self-identified as gay or lesbian. Due to the existing DADT law, the working group was prohibited from identifying and communicating with active duty gay and lesbian members. They hired a private company to conduct those surveys and to protect the identity of gay and lesbian members. The working group also held discussions with various academic, legal, medical, and religious leaders as well as military veterans and members of Congress.

In summary, the report noted the environment in which the military was operating, with wars on several fronts during the previous nine years. U.S. service members and their families were "stretched and stressed" after "multiple and lengthy deployments to Iraq, Afghanistan, and elsewhere" (Report 2010, 1). The immediate environment led opponents of the repeal to question the wisdom of tackling this issue at this time. But the results of the study group were clear and unequivocal:

> [T]he risk of repeal of Don't Ask, Don't Tell to overall military effectiveness is low. We conclude that, while a repeal of Don't Ask, Don't Tell will likely, in the short term, bring about some limited and isolated disruption to unit cohesion and retention, we do not believe this disruption will be widespread or long-lasting, and can be adequately addressed by the recommendations we offer below. Longer term, with a continued and sustained commitment to core values of leadership, professionalism, and respect for all, we are convinced that the U.S. military can adjust and accommodate this change, just as it has others in history. (Report 2010, 3)

A footnote at the end of that statement did add a disclaimer. It noted that the findings of the report were based on the current conditions in the U.S. military. The group's conclusion in support of repealing the policy was not to be construed as doubting the wisdom of enacting the law under the circumstances in 1993. They also noted that a solid 30 percent of those surveyed were opposed to the repeal, with the highest number among the Marines.

A *Washington Post* editorial praised the report for its balanced conclusion:

> The report is remarkable not just for its conclusions but for its honest, thorough and respectful handling of a delicate subject. It offers a clear-eyed, careful, conservative approach to implementing policy change. It doesn't play down the hurdles or denigrate the opposition. It is, in short, a document to be taken seriously, especially by those who may have lingering doubts about allowing gays and lesbians to serve openly. (*Washington Post* 2010)

The *Post* pointed out that the findings showed that military leaders had enough confidence in their institution to integrate openly serving gays similar to how it did previously with blacks and women. It also reiterated the notion that Secretary Gates opined that ending DADT could lead to significant disruption if the courts ordered the integration to occur rather than Congress voting to make it happen.

During the nine months of the study period, the legislative and legal landscape witnessed considerable changes. Efforts to pass the repeal in Congress gained stream in May 2010. A repeal provision was added to the National Defense Authorization Act (NDAA) for Fiscal Year 2011. An amendment that would not have mandated but would have allowed the repeal of DADT upon certification by the president, Secretary of Defense, and Chairman of the Joint Chiefs of Staff that the policy would not harm the military passed the House 234–194 (Keori 2011). The amendment did not come up for a vote in the Senate.

On September 9, 2010, a federal district court in California declared DADT to be unconstitutional in a case brought forth by Log Cabin Republicans in 2004. U.S. district judge Virginia A. Philips ruled that the policy was a violation of First Amendment free speech rights and the Fourteenth Amendment due process for gay service members. The district court issued a worldwide injunction on the policy in October. Justice Department lawyers argued that the judge did not have the authority to issue the injunction. The Obama administration continued to appeal the decision until the congressional vote and presidential signature to end the DADT policy.

State Actors

State governments were not major actors in this debate except through the National Guard. In a high profile case, Col. Margarethe "Grethe" Cammermeyer was dishonorably discharged from the Washington State National Guard in 1992. Cammermeyer disclosed during an interview for top-secret clearance in 1989 that she was a lesbian. She was the highest-ranking official to be dismissed from her position under the DADT policy. Cammermeyer challenged her dismissal and was reinstated by a federal court in 1994. She was allowed to serve as an openly gay person until her retirement in 1997 after thirty-one years of military service and with full military honors (Cammermeyer, nd).

Starting with Massachusetts in 2003, some state governments began legalizing same-sex marriages. As more states affirmed both civil unions and same-sex marriages, it started to raise the issue of gay rights through the federal system.

Further, the U.S. Supreme Court invalidated the Texas law banning consensual sodomy in the case of *Lawrence and Garner v. Texas* (2003). This also struck down similar laws in other states that criminalized some homosexual behavior. The *Lawrence* case, which overturned the *Bowers v. Hardwick* (1986) case, emboldened gay rights advocates. With a legal victory in the courts and greater legal legitimacy under state laws, the push to take on other federal restrictions like DADT escalated.

Political Entrepreneurs and Policy Networks

There were select members of Congress like Reps. Meehan, Tauscher, Murphy, Barney Frank (D-MA), and Jared Polis (D-CO) and Senators Kirsten Gillibrand (D-NY) and Lieberman, among others, who had a particular interest in fighting for the repeal of DADT. Also, President Obama and former President Clinton led the rhetorical charge as well as former military and political leaders.

In November 2007, on the fourteenth anniversary of the law's existence, a letter signed by twenty-eight retired Admirals and Generals was sent to Congress urging repeal of DADT. The military leaders claimed data showed there were 67,000 gay and lesbian members of the armed forces at the time and more than one million gay veterans (Shanker and Healy 2007).

This came after former Chairman of the Joint Chiefs of Staff Gen. John M. Shalikashvili wrote an Op-Ed published in the *New York Times* in January 2007 saying that his conversations with military personnel prompted him to favor overturning DADT.

A group of seventy-seven members of the House of Representatives, led by Alcee Hastings (D-FL), wrote an open letter to President Obama in June 2009 calling for his leadership on repeal of DADT as promised in his campaign. Jared Polis led another group of sixty-eight House members that sent a letter to Obama in September 2010 asking the administration to stop appealing Judge Philip's ruling and to allow an end to DADT (Terkel 2011).

Even former Senator Barry Goldwater (R-AZ) got into the debate. The 1964 Republican candidate for president and retired Major General wrote a letter that was published in the *Washington Post* supporting the right of opening gay members to serve. "You don't have to be 'straight' to fit and die for your country. You just need to shoot straight," Goldwater wrote (Clymer 1998). Goldwater, considered a father of the modern conservative movement in the United States, had a gay grandson, which influenced his public position.

Lt. Dan Choi was one of the most outspoken critics of DADT. In March 2010, Choi handcuffed himself to a White House fence in protest to the policy and was arrested. Choi, a West Point graduate who was fluent in Arabic and served as an infantry platoon leader in Iraq in 2006 and 2007, became a vocal advocate of overturning DADT, and when he announced his sexual orientation on a cable television show, the Army began proceedings to discharge him. Choi was a founding member of a group called Knights Out, an advocacy and education group for LGBT West Point graduates. In July 2010, Lt. Choi was honorably discharged from the National Guard. "Remaining silent when our family and community members are fired or punished for who they truly are would be an unequivocal moral dereliction that tarnishes the honor of the uniform and insults the meaning of America," Choi said (CNN 2010).

Interest Group Involvement

Human Rights Campaign played a critical advocacy role in pushing for the overturning DADT. HRC members and supporters sent more than 625,000 emails and almost fifty thousand handwritten messages to members of Congress urging a vote to overturn the ban (HRC nd).

Two other influential gay rights groups were Servicemembers Legal Defense Network, a legal services group that represented discharged service members, and OutServe, which was an underground group during the legislative battles of 2010 but in 2011 emerged as a leading advocate for gay troops. OutServe claimed to represent about one thousand active duty gay service members. Knights Out represented gay and lesbian alumni, staff, and faculty from West Point. Knights Out estimated there to be 65,000 gays in the military during the debate over repealing the policy. Another advocacy group, the Palm Center from University of California at Santa Barbara, studied how militaries in other countries integrated gay troops. While these groups all agreed on their desire to see an end to the DADT policy, they had disagreements among them on how to proceed with legislative strategy (O'Keefe 2010).

The Servicemembers network organized a project called "Stories From the Front Lines" where they promoted the sending of letters from active duty, veterans, and family members to President Obama to describe the human impact of the DADT policy. In July 2012, Servicemembers Legal Defense Network and OutServe merged their lobbying efforts to push both the legislative and executive branches for greater access to benefits and an end to the Defense of Marriage Act (DOMA) that barred gay couples from receiving full military benefits. The combined organization claimed a donor network of more than 100,000 supporters and to be able to reach more than five thousand active duty, reserve, and National Guard troops (O'Keefe 2012).

Another advocacy group called Citizens For Repeal contacted the Pentagon during the Working Group's study period asking it to allow gay and lesbian troops openly to be heard and named in the report without fear of retribution.

Public Opinion and Polling

There were numerous poll questions asked on support for and against DADT throughout the 1990s and 2000s. Public opinion on the issue of gays serving in the military and support for the repeal of the ban basically gained steam from the time DADT was implemented in 1993.

One study suggests that the rationale for keeping a ban on homosexual service members was twofold. First, there was a belief among many military and political leaders that the public's view of the military as an institution would be harmed if openly gay members were allowed to serve. Second, the argument was advanced that allowing gay service members would harm troop cohesion. Both of these reasons were bolstered by public views of homosexuality as socially unacceptable or, worse, as a disease, a mental disorder, or even as a sin up through the 1960s. But as the modern homosexual rights movement launched with the Stonewall riots in 1969, the advancement of gay pride parades, and an active political agenda in the 1970s, these arguments started to break down (Singer 2008).

There are three general public positions that can be gleaned from polls on the DADT policy: permissive, restrictive, and prohibitive (McCabe 2010). The permissive position maintains that gays should be allowed to openly serve in the military. The restrictive position supports the DADT policy of allowing gays to serve as long as they did not disclose their sexual orientation. The prohibitive position states that gays should not be allowed to serve in the military at all.

ABC News/Washington Post tracked this issue on an annual basis from 1993–2010, specifically framing the questions from the permissive and the prohibitive perspectives. In 1993, they found 44 percent of those polled were for gays openly serving in the military. That number rose to 62 percent in 2001 and 75 percent in 2008 (Guskin 2008). It remained at 75 percent in February 2010 shortly after President Obama called for the repeal of DADT in his State of the Union Address and the Defense Department started its study (O'Keefe and Agiesta 2010).

A CNN poll in November 2010 showed 72 percent in favor of permitting openly gay or lesbian people serving in the military while 23 percent were opposed and 5 percent had no opinion. That was above the already strong 67 percent approval in September and 69 percent in February 2010. The opposition was at 28 percent in September and 27 percent in February. The numbers demonstrated a significant jump from the previous decade. In October 1998, a CNN poll showed 52 percent in favor, 39 percent opposed, and 9 percent with no opinion, while in June 1994, CNN found 53 percent in favor, 41 percent opposed, and 6 percent with no opinion (CNN Opinion 2010).

Even earlier polls cited by the 1992 GAO report showed shifts in public opinion. A national Gallup poll from March 1991 found that 69 percent of those surveyed felt that homosexuals should be allowed to serve in the military compared to 51 percent approval in 1977. Polls by Penn and Schoen Associates, Inc. also found majority support for gays serving in the armed forces (GAO Report 1992).

A 2006 Zogby poll found that 37 percent of personnel serving in Iraq and Afghanistan opposed repealing DADT. At the same time, 45 percent answered that they suspected they were serving with a homosexual. Meanwhile 23 percent reported they were certain they were serving with a homosexual and 59 percent were certain because the gay person had told them directly (Daum 2009).

The winning entry of The Secretary of Defense National Security Essay Competition for 2009 made the case against the argument that homosexual service members weakened force cohesion. Air Force Col. Om Prakash wrote "The Efficacy of 'Don't Ask, Don't Tell'" while he was a student at the Army War College. The essay, which was published in Joint Forces Quarterly and reviewed by Admiral Mullen while he was chairman of the Joint Chiefs of Staff, argues that homosexual service members who compromise their personal integrity by keeping their sexuality secret is damaging to unit cohesion. Prakash cited the examples of Australia, Britain, Canada, and Israel, countries that lifted their bans on gays in the military without witnessing any impact on cohesion, readiness, or performance (Prakash 2009). While not an outright endorsement of ending DADT, the publication of the article signalized a willingness of military leaders to engage in a policy debate about the repeal of the ban on open homosexuals serving in the armed forces.

The Comprehensive Review report found mixed but generally positive results in its survey of service members. The survey was sent to nearly 400,000 service members spilt nearly even between active duty and reserve forces. Their response rate was 29 percent with 115,052 members completing the survey. Of this sample, 30 percent felt that repealing DADT would have no effect specifically on unit effectiveness while 17 percent felt it would be positive, 20 percent felt it would be negative, and 33 percent felt it could be equally positive or negative (Report 2010, 65). Taken together, the mounting public support nationally for repealing DADT emboldened policy officials to act.

THE POLICY PROCESS

Policy Identification

The agenda-setting process for both the 1993 DADT policy and the 2010 repeal of DADT were put in place by Democratic Party politicians, liberal media sources, and gay rights advocacy groups. The issue got on the agenda due to it being raised during the 1992 presidential campaign, and Clinton initiated the process. It reemerged during the 2008 Democratic primary process when candidates made it an issue and also was asked about in primary debates. In both cases, movements had begun in Congress among Democratic House members to pass legislation in support of gays openly serving in the military.

Policy Formation

The old saying goes that Congress proposes and the president disposes of policy proposals. On DADT, both for its initial implementation and for its repeal, the president is primarily the one who is credited for proposing the policies. Congress is responsible for making legislative policy including on military matters. The president can issue executive orders especially related to troop strength through his role as commander-in-chief. In this case, because the policy dealt with military morale, recruiting, and troop readiness, recommendations from military personnel were vital. President Obama requested Secretary Gates to order a comprehensive review of DADT. Gates and Mullin wrote a letter to Representative Ike Skelton (R-MO), Chairman of the Armed Service Committee dated April 30, 2010, stating that they strongly opposed legislation to repeal DADT until the review was complete. The report was completed in nine months, but while the military was studying the issue, some Democratic members of Congress proceeded with introducing proposals and worked to build coalitions to vote to repeal DADT.

The bill that ultimately passed Congress was shaped in House legislation starting in 2006 and finalized with language in the House in May 2010. It took until December to get enough votes in the Senate to pass the bill.

The repeal would only go into effect after the Secretary of Defense, Chairman of the Joint Chiefs, and the president certified that the repeal would not harm troop readiness or military performance. President Obama announced that requirement was met on July 22, 2011. That started the clock for the 60-day countdown to the official repeal.

Policy Adoption

President Obama and Democratic leaders saw an opening to get the controversial issue passed during a lame duck session of Congress in December 2010. Lawmakers were also dealing with a series of other major items, some of who were retiring and others had already lost their reelection campaigns in the midterm elections.

In the Senate, Republicans were able to threaten a filibuster on votes to the NDAA that included the repeal of DADT. Throughout 2010, Majority Leader Harry Reid and Democrats were unable to break the filibuster threat. Lieberman stated in November that he had sixty votes to get past the filibuster. But on December 1, all forty-two Republicans signed a letter to Reid stating that they would halt all Senate business until there was a vote on extending the tax cuts that were set to expire at the end of 2010. On December 9, Republicans voted to block the DADT repeal with a 57–40 tally. Senators Gillibrand, Collins, Lieberman, and Udall introduced standalone legislation and Leader Reid used Senate rules to advance the bill. Under Rule 14, Reid was able to expedite the standalone legislation to prevent it from dying in committee. The bill ended up with forty-four Senate co-sponsors. The House voted for the standalone bill by 250–175 on December 15. Then, on December 18, the Senate passed the standalone bill by a 65–31 vote (Keori 2011).

Policy Implementation

Once Congress passed the repeal, the military immediately prepared to take ownership and implement the new policy. Implementation was left to the Department of Defense and the president. President Obama signed the bill allowing for the repeal of DADT on December 22, 2010. The law required the president, Secretary of Defense, and Chairman of the Joint Chiefs of Staff to certify that the military was ready for the repeal. The repeal would not take place until sixty days after that certification was issued (Keori 2011). The certification signed by Secretary Leon Panetta, Admiral Mullen, and Obama was issued on July 22. On September 20, 2011, at the end of the sixty-day waiting period, DADT was officially repealed.

The official end of DADT was celebrated by its proponents with the release of a book by Aaron Belkin, the director of the Palm Center, and a documentary on HBO. Belkin's book, titled *How We Won: Progressive Lessons from the Repeal of Don't Ask, Don't Tell,* describes how in order to convince Congress to repeal DADT the gay community first needed to persuade the American people that the policy change would not undermine military readiness or effectiveness (Belkin 2011). The HBO movie *The Strange Life of Don't Ask, Don't Tell* documented the seventeen years of the DADT policy and particularly the final fifteen months the law was in effect with interviews of legislators, Pentagon personnel, and actively serving homosexual service members whose identity was obscured because the policy was still in place. A basic premise of both of these works was that the conservative argument that allowing openly homosexual members to serve would damage unit cohesion was a talking point based on a misrepresentation of the truth and not on any factual data.

Soon after the ban was lifted, a book of first-person stories, edited by an active duty Air Force officer and co-founder of OutServe, was published and the results of an online survey conducted by the interest group were released. Their non-scientific survey of more than five hundred currently serving homosexuals found that nearly 40 percent of the respondents planned to "come out" to some of the people with whom they served, including 13 percent saying they would tell everyone about their sexuality while 9 percent said they would tell most of the people in their unit and 17 percent said they would inform some people about their identity (Dao 2011).

After the repeal of DADT, gay and lesbian service members that were previously discharged were granted the opportunity to re-enlist. Numbers on re-enlistees were not readily available nor were numbers on openly gay people who enlisted in the U.S. armed forces after the September 2011 official end of the DADT policy.

A bill to "restore honor" to service members dismissed under DADT was introduced in the 113th Congress in both the House (H.R. 2839) and the Senate (S. 1956). The House bill was referred to the subcommittee on Military Personnel and the Senate bill to the Committee on Armed Services. The legislation would allow for appropriate reviews before military record correction boards or discharge review boards for people dismissed from the military in violation of the DADT policy.

Policy Evaluation

Evaluation of policies that allow service by openly gay and lesbian troops will be an ongoing process. A report by the pro-repeal interest group Palm Center in 2012 found no negative impact on military readiness, unit cohesion, or recruitment and retention of service members from the implementation of the new policy. The Palm Center report was based on interviews with sixty-two active duty service members. Opponents of the repeal, including Senator McCain, were largely unwilling to participate in the survey (Serwer 2012). The study found just two verifiable cases of resignations linked to the policy change and both were military chaplains. The Palm Center claimed that, on balance, the DADT repeal enhanced military readiness and had no effect on retention and recruitment (Glueck 2012).

Secretary Panetta commented that he thought the issue was behind the military and they had moved on. "It's not impacting on morale. It's not impacting on unit cohesion. It is not impacting on readiness. Very frankly, my view is that the military has kind of moved beyond it" (Serwer 2012).

THE ROAD AHEAD/FOLLOW-UP IN CONGRESS

With the repeal of DADT, there were some logistical issues to work through in terms of benefits, marriage, and other policies related to civil liberties of homosexual troops. On September 30, 2011, the Department of Defense announced a policy that permitted military chaplains to perform same-sex marriages in states where they were legal.

In June 2013, the Supreme Court ruled on the Defense of Marriage Act. The Court ruled that the federal restrictions on marriage passed in 1996 by a Republican-led Congress and signed by then-President Clinton were unconstitutional. One immediate consequence was to allow benefits for same-sex couples to be honored even in states that had bans on same-sex marriage.

Even after the repeal of DADT, there was still Article 125 of the Uniform Code of Military Justice that criminalized intimacy between same-sex couples. This portion of the law was a target of gay rights proponents throughout 2011 and 2012. After the Supreme Court struck down the anti-sodomy laws of the states in 2003, DADT was repealed in 2010, and DOMA was found to be unconstitutional in 2013, the anti-sodomy provision in the UCMJ was largely unenforceable. This provision was repealed in the 2014 NDAA as part of sweeping changes to the code.

President Obama was able to use his signing of the law to repeal DADT as a campaign issue in 2012 to appeal to the Democratic and liberal independent bases. The next issue for Obama to address was to move toward support for same-sex marriage, which he started in the 2012 campaign. In an interview with Robin Roberts of ABC News, Obama articulated a more accommodating position but not one of outright support. He said he did not oppose same-sex marriage, but did not endorse it as a policy for the nation.

However, the 2012 GOP platform included a veiled reference to the party's objection to the repeal of DADT. "We reject the use of the military as a platform for social experimentation and will not accept attempts to undermine military priorities and mission readiness" (Republican Platform 2012). Socially conservative candidates like Michele Bachmann, Rick Perry, Rick Santorum, and Newt Gingrich called for reviewing the repeal or even re-imposing the ban.

But 2012 GOP presidential candidate Mitt Romney and Rep. Paul Ryan (R-WI), the vice presidential candidate, did not make DADT an issue. Ryan said he did not think the timing of the repeal was right when he voted against it in December 2010. But, in 2012, he said, "I think the issue is past us. It's done. And I think we need to move on" (Johnson 2012). Romney, the former governor of Massachusetts, a state that allows same-sex marriage, resisted repeated inquires to support a position on reinstating the policy (Glueck 2012).

In the book *Duty* about his time as Secretary of Defense for both George W. Bush and for Obama, Gates underscored Obama's importance in getting DADT repealed while criticizing Obama's overall lack of passion for military affairs. Gates wrote that, "the only military matter, apart from leaks, about which I ever sensed deep passion on his part was 'Don't Ask, Don't Tell.' For him, changing the law seemed to be the inevitable next step in the civil rights movement" (Henry 2014).

As the U.S. armed forces focused on winding down military campaigns in Iraq and Afghanistan during the second decade of the twenty-first century, it appeared to smoothly implement the legal end of discrimination against openly gay and lesbian members serving. The military has served as a platform for social experimentation before with the racial integration of troops after World War II. It seemed that the policy allowing openly homosexual members to serve in the military did not impact unit cohesion, troop readiness, or recruitment efforts. Despite conservative opposition to the repeal, the policy implementation seems to be successful.

NOTES

The author would like to thank David Zaret, a student at Barry University, who contributed research and ideas on the writing of this chapter.

1. Homosexual acts were illegal in every state except Illinois through 1969 and through the Stonewall riots in New York City, which are commonly called the start of the modern gay rights movement.
2. Lieberman endorsed his close friend McCain (R) in the 2008 presidential election over Obama (D).

REFERENCES

Adam, Barry D. 1995. *The Rise of a Gay and Lesbian Movement*. New York: Twayne.

Baker, Peter. 2010. "Powell Favors Repeal of 'Don't Ask, Don't Tell.'" *New York Times*, February 3.

Belkin, Aaron. 2011. "How We Won: Progressive Lessons from the Repeal of Don't Ask, Don't Tell." *Huffington Post*, September 10.

Burrelli, David F., and Judy Feder. 2009. "Homosexuals and the U.S. Military: Current Issues." *Congressional Research Service*, July 22.

Cammermeyer, Grethe. Nd. Biography. *Breaking the Silence*. www.cammermeyer.com/bio.htm.

Cave, Damien. 2006. "Gerry Studds Dies at 69; First Openly Gay Congressman." *New York Times*, October 15.

Clinton, William Jefferson. 1993. The President's News Conference, January 29.

CNN Opinion Research Poll. 2010. CNN Opinion Research Corporation, November 11–14.

CNN Wire Staff. 2010. "Outspoken Gay Soldier Discharged from Army." *CNN.com*, July 23.

Clymer, Adam. 1998. "Barry Goldwater, Conservative and Individualist, Dies at 89." *New York Times*, May 29.

Dao, James. 2011. "Don't Ask, Don't Tell Ends This Week with Celebrations, Revelations, and Questions." *New York Times*, September 19.

Daum, Meghan. 2009. "Writing an End to the Policy of 'Don't Ask, Don't Tell?" *Los Angeles Times*, October 8.

Fox News. 2008. "100 Generals, Admirals Call for Repeal of 'Don't Ask, Don't Tell' Policy on Gays." November 17.

Generals and Admirals Request. 2008. Palm Center. www.palmcenter.org/generals-admirals-request.

GI Hotline. 2011. "'Don't Ask, Don't Tell' Officially Ends on September 20: What Will (and Won't) Change." August 8.

Glueck, Katie. 2012. "Study: 'Don't Ask, Don't Tell' Repeal Hasn't Hurt Military." *Politico*, September 10.

Government Accounting Office. 1992. "Homosexuals in the Armed Forces." United States GAO Report, June 12.

Guskin, Emily. 2008. "Attitudes Toward 'Don't Ask, Don't Tell' Policy Radically Change." *ABC News*, July 19.

Henry, Ed. 2014. "Gates: 'Don't Ask, Don't Tell' Fight Was Only Time Obama Showed 'Passion' for Military Issues." *Fox News*, January 12.

HRC. Nd. "Repeal of 'Don't Ask, Don't Tell," Human Rights Campaign Resources. http://www.hrc.org/resources/entry/the-repeal-of-dont-ask-dont-tell.

Johnson, Luke. 2012. "Paul Ryan: Reserving 'Don't Ask, Don't Tell' Repeal Would Be 'Step In The Wrong Direction.'" *Huffington Post*, September 24.

Keori. 2011. "A Recent History of "Don't Ask, Don't Tell" Repeal." *Daily Kos*, June 27.

McCabe, Brian. 2010. "Public Opinion on 'Don't Ask, Don't Tell.'" *New York Times*, November 30.

Military Readiness Enhancement Act of 2005. H.R. 1059. 109th Congress. Thomas.gov.

National Gay and Lesbian Task Force. Nd. "Discrimination in the Military." http://www.thetaskforce.org/issues/nondiscrimination/military.

O'Keefe, Ed. 2010. "'Don't Ask, Don't Tell' Splitting Gay Rights Groups." *Washington Post*, November 15.

O'Keefe, Ed. 2012. "Gay-rights Groups That Fought 'Don't Ask, Don't Tell' To Merge for Lobbying Efforts." *Washington Post*, July 3.

O'Keefe, Ed, and Jennifer Agiesta. 2010. "75% Back Letting Gays Serve Openly." *Washington Post*, February 12.

Prakash, Om. 2009. "The Efficacy of 'Don't Ask, Don't Tell.'" *Journal Forces Quarterly* 55:88-94.

Report of the Comprehensive Review of the Issues Associated with a Repeal of "Don't Ask, Don't Tell," 2010. Department of Defense. November 30, 1.

Republican Platform. 2012. *We Believe in America*. Committee on Arrangements for the 2012 Republican National Convention.

Ring, Trudy. 2013. "Discharged Gay Service Members to Get Full Separation Pay." *Advocate.com*, January 7.

Serwer, Adam. 2012. "Study: No Negative Impact From DADT Repeal." *Mother Jones*, September 10.

Shalikashvili, John M. 2009. "Data Must Rule the Debate on Gays in the Military." *Washington Post*, June 19.

Shanker, Thom, and Patrick Healy. 2007. "A New Push to Roll Back 'Don't Ask, Don't Tell.'" *New York Times*, November 30.

Shilts, Randy. 2005. *Conduct Unbecoming: Gays and Lesbians in the U.S. Military*. New York: St. Martin's.

Singer, P.W. 2008. "How The Real World Ended 'Don't Ask Don't Tell," Policy Paper, Brookings Institution. Number 6, August.

Terkel, Amanda. 2011. "Jared Polis Announced Birth of Son, Becoming First Openly Gay Parent in Congress." *Huffington Post*, September 30.

Volsky, Igor. 2010. "McCain's Top 11 Positions on 'Don't Ask, Don't Tell.'" *Think Progress*, November 16.

Washington Post Editorial. 2010. "Ready for Change." *Washington Post*, December 1.

Weiner, Tim. 1998. "Military Discharged of Homosexuals Soar." *New York Times*, April 7.

Whitlock, Craig, and Greg Jaffe. 2010. "Pentagon Supports Ending 'Don't Ask, Don't Tell' Law for Gays in Military." *Washington Post*, February 3.

FOUR

The Patient Protection and Affordable Care Act (2010)

Douglas M. Brattebo

On March 23, 2010, President Barack Obama signed into law the Patient Protection and Affordable Care Act (widely known as the Affordable Care Act, or just the ACA, or "Obamacare"). Thus did the United States become the last Western democratic country to enact something approaching a guarantee of universal healthcare access for its population. Embodying a principle long advocated by many Americans on the political left, plus more than a few in the center and some on the right, this new law capped a hundred-year effort, tracing to the Progressive Movement at the outset of the twentieth century, to ensure healthcare access for all Americans. Although several American presidents (most notably Harry Truman, Jimmy Carter, and Bill Clinton) had tried but failed to enact such a law, Obama succeeded—by a hair's breadth, and in an intensely divisive political environment. Whereas earlier watershed pieces of legislation that served as the basis of the modern social welfare state (principally the Social Security Act of 1935 and the laws ushering in both Medicare and Medicaid in 1965) had secured support from legislators of both political parties, the ACA passed both houses of Congress without a single Republican vote. Moreover, the law soon became the object of the intense ire of "tea party" conservatives, whose antics at town hall meetings in the summer of 2010 undercut the law's public support.

Through the four-plus years since its enactment, the ACA has struggled due to a dysfunctional Congress that has not sought to fine-tune the law, a badly botched rollout by the Department of Health and Human Services of the national healthcare exchange (the main online portal through which Americans price, compare, and purchase health plans under the ACA), and lukewarm public opinion about the law because it is perceived by different sectors of the populace as having gone too far or not nearly far enough. Yet by mid-April 2014, just shy of thirteen million previously uninsured Americans had secured health insurance coverage through the ACA: 8.1 million people through the national and state healthcare exchanges and 4.8 million more through the expansion of Medicaid provided for by the law (Editorial Board 2014). Still another three million Americans under the age of twenty-six had been added to their parents' health insurance plans (Editorial Board 2014). The political landscape by summer 2014 indicated that the ACA was in place for the long run, but that seemed to be the only thing certain about its future.

This chapter will address the following seven questions about the Affordable Care Act: (1) What are the main reforms that the ACA made to the United States healthcare system? (2) Why did comprehensive healthcare reform come to the top of the political agenda at the beginning of the Obama administration? (3) Why did such legislation pass this time around, when it had died several times before over a period of many decades? (4) Why did the bill pass without any Republican votes in the House and Senate? (5) How has implementation of the law proceeded thus far? (6) When is Congress likely to begin to work with the current president or one of his successors to modify and improve the functioning of the reforms put in place by the ACA? (7) What is likely to be the standing and reputation of the ACA decades from now?

THE CORE OF COMPLEXITY: THE MOST IMPORTANT CONTENT OF THE AFFORDABLE CARE ACT

Legislation drawn up to reform healthcare in the United States, a sector that makes up more than one-sixth of the country's economy, can be neither simple nor concise. The text of the Affordable Care Act itself runs 955 pages, with the title page and table of contents adding another nineteen pages (Department of Health and Human Services 2010). Helpfully, the Henry J. Kaiser Family Foundation (2012) has summarized the five main provisions of the ACA as follows:

- The Medicaid expansion to 138 percent of the federal poverty level ($15,415 for an individual and $31,809 for a family of four in 2012) for individuals under age sixty-five;
- The creation of health insurance exchanges through which individuals who do not have access to public coverage or affordable employer coverage will be able to purchase insurance with premium and cost-sharing credits available to some people to make coverage more affordable;

- New regulations on health plans that will prevent insurers from denying coverage to people for any reason, including health status, and from charging higher premiums based on health status and gender;
- The requirement that most individuals have insurance beginning in 2014; and
- The penalties to employers that do not offer affordable coverage to their employees, with exceptions for small employers.

A brief word about each of these provisions is in order. With respect to Medicaid expansion, the federal government agreed to pay the cost of newly eligible Medicaid recipients at the rate of 100 percent for 2014-2016, 95 percent for 2017, 94 percent for 2018, 93 percent for 2019, and 90 percent for 2020 and all future years. The national and state online healthcare exchanges offer a forum where Americans without healthcare insurance can compare the content and price of insurance plans that meet a minimum set of standards and then purchase a plan. Healthcare insurance premiums are subsidized, on a sliding scale, for families earning 100 to 400 percent of the federal poverty level ($23,050 to $92,200 for a family of four in 2012); depending on income, this subsidy could limit a policyholder's share of the actual insurance premium cost to anywhere between 2 and 9.5 percent of household income. In addition to not denying anyone coverage for any reason, healthcare plans sold on the exchanges must meet a set of stringent criteria, preventing the previously widespread practice of selling "junk insurance" (insurance laden with fine print provisions designed to ensure that it pays for far fewer contingencies than buyers are led to believe); premiums can vary only on the basis of age, geographical area, tobacco use, and the number of family members; young adults are allowed to remain on a parent's insurance up until they turn twenty-six; there is no lifetime limit on coverage, and coverage can only be rescinded in response to fraud; and insurance companies must spend at least 80 percent of premiums on medical costs—or pay rebates to policyholders if this does not occur. Individuals who do not obtain health insurance will have to pay a penalty of "the greater of $695 per person (up to a maximum of $2,085 per family), or 2.5 percent of household income," to be phased in from 2014–2016 (Henry J. Kaiser Family Foundation 2012). Finally, "employers with more than fifty employees will be assessed a fee of $2,000 per full-time employee (in excess of thirty employees)" if not providing coverage for employees and if at least one employee receives a premium credit through an exchange; employers that offer coverage and have fifty or more employees also are required to automatically enroll employees into the "lowest cost premium plan if the employee does not sign up for employer coverage or does not opt out of coverage" (Henry J. Kaiser Family Foundation 2012).

The Affordable Care Act sought to increase the percentage of Americans with quality health insurance, reflecting the consensus of healthcare experts that, unless and until all or very nearly all Americans possess such insurance, it will be challenging to produce better healthcare outcomes for the population or to contain the explosive growth in healthcare costs over recent decades. The Congressional Budget Office (2013) estimated that the ACA would increase the portion of Americans with healthcare insurance from 82 percent in 2013 to 92 percent in 2023. This calculation projected an increase by 2023 of 13 million in the number of Americans to gain coverage through Medicaid, and an increase of 24 million in the number of Americans to gain coverage through the national and state exchanges (Congressional Budget Office 2013). For reasons to be explored later in this chapter, however, the expansion of Medicaid provided for by the ACA will occur significantly more slowly than projected, although the number of Americans gaining coverage through the national and state exchanges appears on track to meet or exceed the CBO's projections.

To put it mildly, the enactment of the ACA was a big deal—medically, socially, economically, and politically—in the unfolding of the American experience. Or, as Vice President Joseph Biden attempted to whisper to President Obama within recording distance of microphones on March 23, 2010, at the signing ceremony for the ACA: "This is a big fucking deal!" (Adams 2010). Even conceding the accuracy of Biden's colorful characterization, it is important to recall that in the American policymaking context, doing big things is rare, and backlash and complications can ensue from the passage of momentous legislation, no matter how necessary and appropriate.

THAT OLD FAMILIAR FEELING: HEALTHCARE REFORM RETURNS TO THE TOP OF THE POLITICAL AGENDA

The Constitution of the United States was not designed to maximize legislative efficiency; neither was it constructed to streamline the functioning of government in general. Among the facets sewn into the document are principles of separation of powers, checks and balances, and bicameralism that make it hard for the country to enact historic legislative policy shifts in one big swoop. The Constitution thus is quite effective at preventing tyranny and limiting the reach of government into every nook of Americans' lives, but it also regularly frustrates those Americans who would prefer public policy issues to be addressed promptly and comprehensively. It is the norm that the country legislates in piecemeal, in dribs and drabs, inching forward to address a particular policy challenge. This requires great patience, and even faith, that policy logjams will eventually break if enough Americans have wanted something intensely over a long time and struggled to bring it into being. As David Brian Robertson put it in *The Constitution and America's Destiny*:

> [M]aking this national policy process work requires very broad-based political coalitions and sustained, concerted efforts. To use this government, Americans must engage in politics. They must build and sustain the large political coalitions necessary to align the House, the Senate, the presidency, the courts, and a large number of states. Building coalitions requires understanding the interests of many different kinds of people, locating a common set of objectives that can motivate their continuing cooperation, and working constantly to anticipate and remedy the endless, inevitable conflicts that threaten their cooperative effort. (Robertson 2005, 264–65)

The fact that the country is able to do its biggest legislative things only when many conditions align has drawn the attention of scholars. In his important book, *Agendas, Alternatives, and Public Policies*, John W. Kingdon sought "to understand why some subjects become prominent on the policy agenda and others do not, and why some alternatives for choice are seriously considered and others are neglected" (Kingdon 1984, 3). Kingdon theorized persuasively that a "policy window" opens when three largely independent streams (problems, policies, and politics) converge to create a brief opportunity for action on a particular proposal. Regarding *problems*, it is true that some come to the attention of policymakers and the broader public through individual and institutional efforts to monitor certain issues, but it is also true that "focusing events" sometimes boost a particular problem to prominence. These moments of clarity, often marked by an air of crisis, can create a consensus that something needs to be done. At such times, when a problem rises to general attention, proposals of *policies*—generated, revised, and nurtured by policy communities of experts in government, higher education, private industry, and think tanks until the moment is right—suddenly make their way into the mainstream. Civil servants utilize these policy proposals in crafting specific policy alternatives with which politicians can work. The prospect that any one of these policies will be enacted depends on how *politics*—the manner in which actors and institutions (public opinion, interest group lobbying efforts, the partisan and ideological balance within Congress, etc.)—are configured at a specific moment. It is elected officials, with the president standing out from the pack, that are then the most important in determining whether and how a particular thing will get done (Kingdon 1984).

Mark Peterson (2011) has summarized quite adeptly why healthcare reform made it to the top of the policy agenda during Obama's presidency, and why the urgency for tangible action was more intense than under previous administrations (F.D. Roosevelt, Truman, Nixon/Ford, Carter, and Clinton) that had taken the lead in seeking to enact comprehensive reform. Using a rubric of three categories, each measured by multiple indicators, Peterson concludes that the *problem* of healthcare had become a national imperative by the time Obama became president. Peterson notes that healthcare cost pressures (as measured by four variables: U.S. healthcare spending relative to that of other countries, inflation of healthcare costs, government spending on healthcare, and business spending on healthcare) had reached the most severe level, across all four variables, out of four gradations of seriousness. The only other time this had happened was during the Clinton presidency. Likewise, healthcare coverage pressures (as measured by individual spending on healthcare; the number of uninsured Americans; the number of underinsured Americans; and the variance of uninsured percentages based on race, ethnicity, or socioeconomic status) also had reached the most severe level, across all four variables, of the four gradations of seriousness. This had never occurred before, with only three out of four variables having reached the most severe level during the Clinton presidency. Finally, consequences (defined as what the healthcare system delivers, and measured by indicators in three categories: healthcare outcomes, the rank of the United States compared to other countries, and the health of the American population) had reached the most severe level in the second category, and the penultimate level in the first and third categories. Here again, things had been less dire during the Clinton presidency, when none of the three categories had reached the most severe level.

Peterson's conclusion is that "compelling evidence of systemwide problems in healthcare across the domains of costs, coverage, and consequences did not emerge until the Clinton administration. By the time of the Obama administration, the evidence was even more pronounced" (Peterson 2011, 431). Moreover, the economic collapse of 2008 crystallized many Americans' worries that they could lose their access to healthcare, without warning, at any time. The economic crisis made health insurance reform a significant topic in the presidential campaigns of Senators Barack Obama (IL) and Hillary Clinton (NY) for the 2008 Democratic presidential nomination. Both candidates put their support behind versions of proposed healthcare reform *policies* that were identical in broad strokes (Hacker 2011).

AGAINST ALL ODDS: CONGRESS ENACTS A LAW

As the term "policy windows" suggests, the moments when the three streams converge are often fleeting. And even then, there is no guarantee that something will get done. Sometimes the window slams shut without warning; other times the opening is narrow to begin with, but this does not dawn on policymakers until it is too late; and still on other occasions the number of proposals under consideration builds up, with no single plan emerging from the pack, and the political system remains paralyzed while the moment for action fades. For a variety of reasons, whenever universal healthcare reform rose to the top of the nation's agenda throughout the twentieth century, no plan could ever get across the finish line to be enacted by Congress. The Affordable Care Act, however, found its way through the policy window, despite repeated prognostications that this would not happen. Why did the Affordable Care Act make its way into law, in defiance of the historical pattern?

As noted earlier, Peterson has documented why healthcare reform had become a high-priority problem in American politics by the time Obama was sworn in as president, and Peterson also has looked at the state of healthcare reform *politics* during the Obama administration as compared with previous periods. Peterson finds that interest groups (as measured by "the unity or collapse of the traditional antireform alliance of organized medicine, other healthcare providers, insurers, and employers, as well as the weak or strong mobilization of interests committed to reform") were positively disposed toward reform at the outset of Obama's presidency, as they were early on under Clinton. However, whereas the Senate under Obama was neutrally configured with respect to healthcare reform just as it had been under Clinton, the House under Obama had become favorably disposed to reform as compared to neutral under Clinton. This gave Obama an important edge, and it was magnified by the facts that he had won a significant majority of the popular vote in the 2008 presidential election, the public still supported healthcare reform (at least as a general principle) during the long legislative process, and Obama could count on a high number of "solid" votes within his own party on healthcare in both legislative chambers. Only FDR had enjoyed greater room for maneuver in the House and Senate, but he had faced greater interest group opposition, and healthcare had not yet risen to the top of the nation's policy agenda, a process that would take the remainder of the twentieth century and nearly the first decade of the twenty-first. Peterson's conclusion, following from the analysis discussed above, is crucial: "There simply was no other time for favorable healthcare reform politics like 2009–2010" (Peterson 2011, 435).

However, as Peterson also points out, Obama made important strategic and tactical decisions that brought legislative action from the realm of the possible into accomplished fact. Peterson praises Obama for two strategic choices and two tactical choices. In terms of strategy, Obama avoided Clinton's mistake of getting too involved in the legislative process, an error embodied by Clinton's empaneling of a working group (led by First Lady Hillary Clinton) to draw up the legislative reform proposal behind closed doors; instead, the formulation of the ACA was "open, fluid, and congressionally based" (Peterson 2011, 436). Obama also negotiated early in the process with "organized medicine and the pharmaceutical and insurance industries" so that they would not oppose the legislation (Peterson 2011, 436), whereas they had worked hard to kill Clinton's Health Security Act in 1993 and 1994. This time around, the industries reasoned that it was better to help craft the legislation than to defeat it (Brown 2011). Tactically, Obama knew that speed was of the essence and thus maneuvered to have both the House and Senate pass their healthcare reform bills by the same point in the process at which Clinton had only introduced his Health Security Act (Peterson 2011, 436). "Final passage for Obama came with a nation divided but not in nearly full retreat, as with Clinton" (Peterson 2011, 436). Obama also sensed that, having invested so much work and political capital in healthcare reform, the Democratic Party could not afford to fail to enact the ACA. The Democrats lost a Senate seat in January 2010 when Republican Scott Brown defeated Martha Coakley in a special election for the remainder of the late Edward Kennedy's term in the Senate. This meant that the Democratic Senate majority was now fifty-nine instead of the filibuster-proof sixty. Obama left it to House Speaker Nancy Pelosi to use her parliamentary expertise and command of the Democratic majority to push the Senate's (admittedly imperfect) version of the ACA through the House (Peterson 2011, 436).

As Lawrence D. Brown has observed, in previous attempts to enact systemic healthcare reform, the Democratic legislative coalition had fractured, but this time, miraculously, it held together (Brown 2011). The fact that there were no Republican votes up for grabs late in the process left Democrats staring into the abyss: either the ACA would pass on the basis of Democratic unity, or it would go down to defeat, meaning that years of hard work would be lost (Brown 2011). The price of disunity was too high to pay, even for many Democratic legislators who were unhappy with various provisions of the ACA. The only thing worse than enacting, without any Republican votes, an imperfect law that already was showing signs of unpopularity with the public, would have been to deliver nothing at all, as had occurred with Clinton's proposed Health Security Act in 1994. Interestingly, public opinion polls in early 2010 showed that the public, despite misgivings about the pending legislation, nevertheless would be "angry" and "disappointed" if it failed (Hacker 2011). If previous attempts were any guide, healthcare reform might not have returned to the top of the political agenda for several or many years.

A ONE-PARTY COALITION: REPUBLICANS ABANDON THEIR FAVORED HEALTHCARE REFORM MODEL

Enactment of the most important piece of healthcare reform legislation since 1965, accomplished with the votes of only one political party, stuck in the craw of the most ideological Republican Congress members and citizens alike, particularly those identifying with the "tea party." The blowback against a law that some Americans inside and outside of Congress perceived and characterized as somehow unfair or illegitimate has continued to taint American politics to the present day. But the reasons why the Affordable Care Act came to be passed without a single Republican vote in Congress tell us far more about the pathologies of the Republican Party than about the ACA or those legislators who supported it.

The rightward ideological lurch of the Republican Party over the past two decades is well known, and the consequences for the capacity of the governmental system to function have been severe. Only if one appreciates this fundamental reality of contemporary American politics is it possible to understand how the Affordable Care Act passed without the support of a single Republican legislator. The antipathy of the contemporary Republican Party to bargaining, negotiating, and compromising with the Democratic Party prevented many Republican members of the House and Senate from voting for a healthcare reform plan that had been devised, promoted, and even implemented within one state, all by Republicans.

Douglas M. Brattebo (2014) has chronicled the Republican Party's strategic dilemma. In a nutshell, the Republican Party's positions on issues have come to be fashioned by the decidedly anachronistic convictions of old white guys in rural areas of the Rocky Mountains, High Plains, and, above all, the Deep South. The GOP adopted in the late 1960s a "southern strategy" based on states' rights, resistance to the mandates of the national government, a zealous dislike of taxation, and hostility to any expansion of the role of government. This strategy worked well in a mostly-white country when a letter L formation of solidly Republican states in the Electoral College, running south from the Canadian border through the Rocky Mountain and Plains states to Texas and then east across the South to the East Coast, made it relatively easy for Republican candidates to win the presidency. The strategy, however, works a lot less well, if at all, in a changing America destined to have a majority non-white population by 2043 in which African-Americans, Asian-Americans, and Latino-Americans have coalesced into the core of a rising electoral coalition that also encompasses women (particularly single women), highly-educated voters, younger voters, and LGBT voters.

The component groups of this new coalition are decidedly not hostile to government, are not afraid to pay taxes, and have an intense dislike of the injection of religious fundamentalism into politics on issue after issue. The rising coalition wants government to work well and embrace policies based on evidence and reason. Insightful Republican strategists see clearly that the party must relinquish its fealty to a small and shrinking base, broaden its policies to appeal to a wider swath of Americans, and participate meaningfully in the process of crafting and enacting legislative solutions through a rediscovered willingness to compromise. All of this, however, is easier said than done. The "tea party" caucus members in the

House, elected from gerrymandered districts with borders that will not change until the next round of redistricting flowing from the 2020 census takes effect in the 2022 midterm elections, are not going anywhere right away. Although extreme conservatives lately have been on the political defensive against the Republican establishment, House Speaker John Boehner (R-OH) and other congressional leaders have found it impossible to reform the party and steer it to the political center at anything approaching the rate necessary to prevent the party from becoming less and less relevant to the lives of most Americans. At this writing, it seems almost a certainty that the Republican Party will gain seats in the House in the 2014 midterm elections. Tragically, this will be taken by the base of the party as proof positive that there is no real urgency to change, thus ensuring that change becomes more difficult with each passing month, and compounding the party's strategic problems in future presidential, and eventually congressional, elections.

There is dumfounding irony in the fact that the Affordable Care Act, both philosophically and in terms of its main legislative framework, was the brainchild of a conservative think tank, the Heritage Foundation, which in 1989 put forward the idea of an individual mandate requiring Americans to purchase health insurance (Gusmano 2013). In 1993, nineteen Republican senators sponsored a bill, the Health Equity and Access Reform Today Act, which contained an individual mandate provision of the sort that Democrats came to embrace in subsequent years (Gusmano 2013). Republican hostility to the notion of an individual healthcare insurance mandate is thus a rather new phenomenon (Gusmano 2013) that may have more to do with "tea party" conservatives' hatred of President Obama than anything else. The erroneous chain of "logic" is simple enough to follow: if President Obama is a Kenyan Muslim Socialist, then his healthcare reform plan must be bad, too, never mind that it is an exceedingly cautious modification springing from the same evidence-based motivations that have stirred all other Western democracies to adopt universal healthcare.

The situation becomes even more curious when one realizes that Republican Mitt Romney, Obama's opponent in the 2012 presidential election, had championed a "conservative" approach to healthcare reform as governor of Massachusetts and signed into law in 2006 an act that became the model for the ACA (Gusmano 2014). The Massachusetts law did indeed emerge as the model for national reform in subsequent years (Brown 2011). Between 2006 and 2012, however, the Republican Party moved so far to the ideological right that what once was a conservative policy approach to healthcare reform now was seen as an unacceptable overreach by the federal government. In 2012, Romney found it necessary to denounce the very state law that he had once expected to use as a template for enacting national healthcare reform if he were to win the White House. Indeed, Romney tried to convince primary voters that the

ACA and the Massachusetts law were not birds of a feather, but these efforts were generally unconvincing (Gusmano 2013).

A BUMPY ROAD: IMPLEMENTATION PROBLEMS APLENTY AND A DO-NOTHING CONGRESS

States controlled by a Republican political establishment sought to prevent the ACA from becoming law, and these same states did everything they could to kill the act by resisting the implementation of the ACA from the moment it was signed into law (Purdum 2013). This hostility manifested itself in a sabotage campaign with three main prongs: resistance to Medicaid expansion; nonparticipation in setting up state healthcare exchanges through which citizens could examine, compare, and purchase health insurance policies; and refusal to inform citizens of such states of their eligibility to purchase health insurance on the national healthcare exchange. The Department of Health and Human Services' incompetent rollout of the national healthcare exchange, which debuted on October 1, 2013, exacerbated the situation.

In *National Federation of Independent Business v. Sebelius* (June 2012), a majority of five Supreme Court justices, led by Chief Justice John Roberts, upheld nearly all of the Affordable Care Act's provisions, including the individual mandate, which the Court found to be constitutional under Congress's power to tax (Gusmano 2013). Crucially and unexpectedly, however, the Court ruled that the federal government could *not* require states to expand Medicaid (Gusmano 2013). Despite the fact that in earlier decades the federal government had compelled states to adopt higher drinking age and mandatory seatbelt laws with the threat of withholding federal money for existing programs, the Roberts Court contended that "the Medicaid expansion was really the creating of a new program. It was too coercive, in [Roberts's] view, for the federal government to threaten funding for the original Medicaid program in order to pressure states to adopt this 'new' Medicaid program" (Gusmano 2013). The Commerce Clause powers of Congress under the Constitution did not extend so far, the Court concluded, thereby lending heft to a conservative cause, which had been building since *Lopez v. United States* (1995) seeking to limit the expansion of the federal government's regulatory powers (Gusmano 2013).

As of this writing, twenty-six states and the District of Columbia were in the process of implementing Medicaid expansion under the ACA, nineteen states had determined not to move forward at this time, and five states were debating whether to do so (Henry J. Kaiser Family Foundation 2014a). Stunningly, approximately five million Americans whom the CBO had expected to gain health insurance right away due to Medicaid expansion under the ACA were kept out of the program (Henry J. Kaiser

Family Foundation 2014a). Leading the pack of nonexpanding states were Texas with more than one million and Florida with more than three-quarters of a million (Henry J. Kaiser Family Foundation 2014a). Gusmano (2013) is almost certainly right that the holdout states are unlikely to abstain forever from joining Medicaid expansion, because the federal aid money at issue is too great to resist and also because holdout state governments will face increasing pressure from their hospitals, nursing homes, and county and city governments to get with the program. In the meantime, however, the cost to these states in dollars, strain on their healthcare institutions, and the health of their citizens will be significant.

Many Republican governors decided not to have their states create healthcare exchanges for their populations, and this required the federal government to assume full or partial responsibility for creating healthcare exchanges for thirty-six states (Purdum 2013). By the summer of 2014, sixteen states and the District of Columbia had established state-based exchanges, seven states had created exchanges in partnership with the federal government, and fully twenty-seven states still had exchanges facilitated by the federal government (Henry J. Kaiser Family Foundation 2014b). Adding insult to injury, "in the months leading up to the program's debut, some states refused to do anything at all to educate the public about the law" (Purdum 2013). Indicative of the resistance in some deeply conservative Republican states to Medicaid expansion was Texas Governor Rick Perry's statement that "Texas will not be held hostage to the Obama administration's attempt to force us into this fool's errand" (Cheney 2013). But, with so much money left on the federal table and Texas's healthcare safety net buckling under the weight of one million uninsured citizens who could be covered by Medicaid if the state would allow it, any dispassionate observer had to wonder whose behavior was, in fact, foolish.

The debut of the national and state online healthcare exchanges on Tuesday, October 1, 2013, was nothing short of calamitous. A high proportion of customers attempting to use HealthCare.gov and a number of the state exchange websites found that they could not create user accounts, compare insurance plans, or find out whether they qualified for federal premiums to help offset the cost of coverage (*New York Times* 2013). The federal exchange essentially collapsed under the weight of 8.6 million unique visitors during its first four days of operation (*New York Times* 2013). Less than a week after the launch of the federal exchange, the Department of Health and Human Services, which had overseen the three-and-one-half-year process of designing HealthCare.gov, conceded that design and software problems were responsible for the debacle and that these huge problems would have to be systemically addressed with breakneck speed (Weaver et al. 2013). Officials at HHS, and some in the White House, had been warned about the inadequacy of the website but had not taken the warnings to heart (LaFraniere and Lipton 2013). By

December 1, two full months after the debut of the healthcare exchanges, HealthCare.gov was finally functioning well for most users (Norman 2013) and it, as well as most state exchanges, continued to improve in subsequent months. In addition to the website fiasco, a series of delays and modifications to the statutorily-mandated timetable for the ACA's implementation played out across 2013 and 2014. Often these deviations seemed to stem from complaints and pressure from consumers or segments of the healthcare industry (Goldstein 2014). Sometimes these variations drew accusations that they were being made solely to protect the political standing of the ACA. When HHS Secretary Kathleen Sebelius resigned her position in early April 2014, the *New York Times* characterized her departure as "ending a stormy five-year tenure marred by the disastrous rollout of President Obama's signature legislative achievement, the Affordable Care Act" (Shear 2014). The Senate confirmed Sylvia Mathews Burwell as Sebelius's successor on June 5, 2014.

LIKE OLD TIMES: WISTFUL FOR A CONGRESS THAT WORKS

By the fourth anniversary of the ACA's enactment, the Republican House had voted fifty-four times to repeal, gut, or otherwise undermine the statute (O'Keefe 2014), a remarkable statistic from a period insightfully dubbed by NBC News as "The Four Years War" (Todd et al. 2013). This cavalcade of votes in the House occurred despite the fact that there was no chance that the Democratic Senate—not to mention President Obama, whose moniker has been attached to what must be considered his defining domestic legislative accomplishment—would participate in undermining the ACA. It was hard to escape the conclusion that one ideological faction within the Republican Party was working awfully hard to deny healthcare coverage to millions of Americans and that, if it could do so, it would be only too happy to undo the ACA altogether. Yet if one listened at all attentively, one could hear the "Repeal!" war cry beginning to recede in political races all across the nation, as a decisive majority of Americans told pollsters that they preferred that the law be "improved rather than repealed" (Editorial Board 2014). Republican candidates were speaking more frequently about "fixing" the ACA and Democratic candidates were beginning to claim credit for the law's benefits (Editorial Board 2014).

There are moments when one is tempted to predict that Congress will start to work with Obama, or his successor, to fine-tune the Affordable Care Act. Such optimism, however, is apt to be premature. "In a normal political environment," President Obama has observed, "it would have been easier for me to simply call up the speaker and say, 'You know what, this is a tweak that doesn't go to the essence of the law . . . it looks like there may be some better ways to do this. Let's make a technical change to the law.' That would be the normal thing I would prefer to do. But we're not in a normal atmosphere around here when it comes to Obamacare" (Purdum 2013). Joseph White (2011) has noted that House Republicans are unlikely, in significant numbers, to become interested in repairing Obamacare any time soon. White also thinks that, should the Democrats somehow regain control of the House before the next redistricting goes into effect, the newly-elected Democratic representatives would hail from competitive districts and see great political peril in spending political capital on revising the Affordable Care Act (White 2011). Beyond 2022, however, perhaps that calculation will change, with not only a different president but also a significant number of representatives elected from redrawn congressional districts. Until then, it is very likely that the law will move ahead as it has done to date: messily, with public ambivalence, but also with a steadily growing number of Americans who have quality health insurance because of it.

That last fact is important, because the next presidential election could well unfold against the backdrop of ongoing ACA implementation that has assisted a total of twenty million or more Americans in obtaining health insurance through the national and state exchanges. Many more Americans, perhaps totaling ten million or more, are likely to have obtained health insurance as additional holdout states succumb to both fiscal and moral logic and decide to join Medicaid expansion. All of this is to say that not only the demographics of the country but also the politics of the ACA are likely to look a lot different in 2016, 2020, and 2024 than they are today. Both trends will contribute to the demise of the "tea party," force the Republican Party, if quite belatedly, to move to the political center, and make it conceivable that even a future president and congressional majority of different political parties will see merit in collaborating to enhance the ACA rather than fighting over whether it should even exist. There could even be (queue dramatic music) . . . meaningful compromise.

Along the road to this scenario, though, another very important development is likely to gather momentum. The attention of policy experts, government officials, and segments of the medical industry will turn to the one great healthcare policy question that the Affordable Care Act purposefully did not address: cost containment. As Brown (2011) has observed, the ACA, just like Romney's Massachusetts law, postponed serious examination of cost control until after the implementation phase. In both instances it was expedient, and perhaps even indispensable, to do so (Hacker 2011). Indeed, there are not yet obvious signs that the public is ready for an earnest conversation about cost, supply, and demand, but as the Independent Medicare Advisory Board begins to exercise its power under the ACA to overturn proposed payment increases, this issue will resurface at some point (Brown 2011). Also, the United States has been fortunate to experience a significant drop in the rate of healthcare price inflation since the enactment of the ACA, and the law actually may bear some credit for the attenuation. At some point, though, this happy trend will give way to renewed inflationary pressures, which will become apparent to all. With access to healthcare dramatically expanded, the main debate will come to be about cost.

IN THE FULLNESS OF TIME: HISTORY'S JUDGMENT OF THE AFFORDABLE CARE ACT

In any democracy, the greatest projects remain unfinished, to be reexamined, debated anew, and addressed again by future generations. Policy challenges have a habit of changing, morphing, and bedeviling. The path to progress always seems uphill, particularly in the American constitutional system, in which difficult things eventually get accomplished but never truly solved. So it is likely to be with the Affordable Care Act, of which Jacob Hacker has observed, "The real question now is whether it will be an isolated achievement or a stepping-stone to more effective reforms" (Hacker 2011, 441). Yet Americans are, in the sweep of history, mere beginners, albeit eager novices who might just yet find a salutary way forward on healthcare policy. It is appropriate to give Peterson the last word:

> Substantively, like the original Medicare statute in 1965, the Affordable Care Act of 2010 is a beginning, not an end. It is a foundation for future reform efforts. Politically, it is the end of the beginning, the terminus of a century-long ideological battle over a national commitment to universal coverage and the crafting of instruments of fiscal discipline and system innovation to make such a commitment possible (Peterson 2011, 436).

REFERENCES

Adams, Richard. 2010. "Joe Biden: 'This Is a Big Fucking Deal.'" *Guardian*, April 23. Accessed June 5, 2014. www.theguardian.com/world/richard-adams-blog/2010/mar/23/joe-biden-obama-big-fucking-deal-overheard.

Brattebo, Douglas M. 2014. "Closed for Repairs So It Can Reengage with the World: Prospects for Reforming the Republican Party." In *The American Election 2012: Contexts and Consequences*, edited by R. Ward Holder and Peter B. Josephson, 21-35. New York: Palgrave Macmillan.

Brown, Lawrence D. 2011. "The Elements of Surprise: How Health Reform Happened." *Journal of Health Politics, Policy and Law* 36: 419–27.

Cheney, Kyle. 2013. "Rick Perry: White House Holding States 'Hostage' with Medicaid Expansion." *Politico*, April 1.

Congressional Budget Office. 2013. "CBO's May 2013 Estimate of the Effects of the Affordable Care Act on Health Insurance Coverage." Accessed June 5, 2014. http://www.cbo.gov/sites/default/files/ cbofiles/attachments/43900-2013-05-ACA.pdf.

Department of Health and Human Services. 2010. "Full Text of the Affordable Care Act and Reconciliation Act." Accessed June 5, 2014. www.hhs.gov/healthcare/rights/law/.

Editorial Board. 2014. "The Vanishing Cry of 'Repeal It.'" *New York Times*, June.

Goldstein, Amy. 2014. "Timeline of Major Changes to the Affordable Care Act." *New York Times*, March 8.

Gusmano, Michael K. 2013. "*NFIB v. Sebelius*: The Political Expediency of the Roberts Court." *Health Economics, Policy and Law* 8: 119–24.

Gusmano, Michael K. 2014. "Health Care in the 2012 Election." In *The Presidential Election of 2012: A Transformation in National Politics*, edited by Douglas M. Brattebo, Tom Lansford, and Jack Covarrubias. Akron, OH: University of Akron Press.

Hacker, Jacob S. 2011. "Why Reform Happened." *Journal of Health Politics, Policy and Law* 36: 437–41.

Henry J. Kaiser Family Foundation. 2012. "Summary of the Coverage Provisions in the Affordable Care Act." Accessed June 5, 2014. kaiserfamilyfoundation.files.wordpress.com/2013/01/8023-r.pdf.

Henry J. Kaiser Family Foundation. 2014. "Status of State Action on the Medicaid Expansion Decision." Accessed June 5, 2014. kff.org/health-reform/state-indicator/state-activity-around-expanding-medicaid-under-the-affordable-care-act/.

Henry J. Kaiser Family Foundation. 2014a. "Interactive: A State-by-State Look at How the Uninsured Fare Under the ACA." Accessed June 5, 2014. kff.org/interactive/uninsured-gap/.

Henry J. Kaiser Family Foundation. 2014b. "State Marketplace Statistics." Accessed June 5, 2014. kff.org/health-reform/state-indicator/state-marketplace-statistics/.

Kingdon, John W. 1984. *Agendas, Alternatives, and Public Policies*. Boston: Little, Brown and Co.

LaFraniere, Sharon, and Eric Lipton. 2013. "Officials Were Warned About Health Site Woes." *New York Times*, November 18.

New York Times. 2013. "Opening Week of Health Exchanges." *New York Times*, October 4.

Norman, Brett. 2013. "White House Site Now Works for 'Vast Majority.'" *Politico*, December 1.

O'Keefe, Ed. 2014. "The House Has Voted 54 Times in Four Years on Obamacare. Here's the Full List." *Washington Post*, March 21.

Peterson, Mark A. 2011. "It Was a Different Time: Obama and the Unique Opportunity for Health Care Reform." *Journal of Health Politics, Policy and Law* 36: 429–36.

Purdum, Todd S. 2013. "The Obamacare Sabotage Campaign." *Politico*, November 1.

Robertson, David Brian. 2005. *The Constitution and America's Destiny*. New York: Cambridge University Press.

Shear, Michael D. 2014. "Sebelius Resigns After Troubles Over Health Site." *New York Times*, April 10.

Todd, Chuck, et al. 2013. "First Thoughts: The Four Years War." *First Read from NBC News*, October 30.

Weaver, Christopher, et al. 2013. "Software, Design Defects Cripple Health-Care Website: Government Acknowledges It Needs to Fix Design and Software Problems." *Wall Street Journal*, October 6.

White, Joseph. 2011. "Muddling Through the Muddled Middle." *Journal of Health Politics, Policy and Law* 36: 443–48.

FIVE

Higher Education Opportunity Act (2008)

Sunil Ahuja

Higher education has become an increasingly regulated entity in the United States. Many regulations come from laws passed at the national and state levels, which seek to define the purposes and provisions of higher education. Chief among them is the Higher Education Act, originally passed in 1965 as part of President Lyndon Johnson's Great Society programs, which has been reauthorized numerous times since then (in 1968, 1971, 1972, 1976, 1980, 1986, 1992, 1998, and 2008).

My purpose in this chapter is to delve into the last reauthorization in 2008. This chapter discusses the passage of the reauthorization in Congress, highlights its key components, and notes what happened during the implementation phase of the law. The chapter is placed in the context of major topics and studies in public policy literature, and concludes with a brief discussion regarding the next reauthorization on the Higher Education Act.

As noted above, higher education has been on the national agenda since 1965. The issue has evolved over time, and different aspects of problem, policy, and political streams have impacted its evolution over time (Kingdon 1995). A variety of actors and events both inside and outside the government have influenced its development, as it happens with the formulation of any public policy (Cobb and Elder 1983; Baumgartner and Jones 1993). In recent years, the formulation as well as implementation of higher education policy has been marred by partisan factors, as noted in the concluding chapter of this book.

PASSAGE IN CONGRESS

After considerable debate and discussion and many delays, the Higher Education Opportunity Act (HEOA), Public Law 110-315, was signed on August 14, 2008, by then President George W. Bush. The delays spanned six years, three congresses, and came after fourteen short-term extensions of the previous reauthorizations. The law is 1,158 pages long; it created about seventy new spending programs and established over one hundred new reporting requirements for higher education institutions.

The bill first passed unanimously in the Senate in August of 2007 (Field 2007d). The Senate's version contained several key provisions, including an increase in maximum allowable Pell Grants from $4,310 to $6,300, an expansion of government's oversight of institutions' tuition-setting policies, and a ban on institutions from using federal dollars to lobby Congress. The key players in the Senate, at this stage, were Senators Ted Kennedy (D-MA) and Tom Coburn (R-OK).

Earlier in the year, the Senate Health, Education, Labor, and Pensions (HELP) Committee moved legislation that would dramatically reduce government subsidies to student-loan companies and increase student aid. The bill also would have significantly increased the amount of regulations for higher education institutions. Senator Lamar Alexander (R-TN), a former university president and U.S. secretary of education, complained that "[t]his bill doubles the amount of regulations and rules for colleges. If we are sending money to colleges and universities, we ought to look after it. But we shouldn't overburden the system with even well-meaning regulations" (qtd. in Field 2007c). The committee approved a "manager's amendment" that relaxed provisions in the bill regarding federal oversight of institutions' transfer-of-credit policies (Field 2007c).

The Senate committee, however, rejected an amendment to create a federal student loan program to compete with private loans. Senator Sherrod Brown (D-OH), who advanced the notion that the government could provide nonguaranteed college loans to students at attractive rates, sponsored the amendment. Opponents, including Senator Michael Enzi (R-WY), the ranking minority member on the Senate Health, Education, Labor, and Pensions Committee, argued that the proposal would give too much power to the Department of Education, which presumably would be in charge of determining the interest rates for the program. Finally, among other amendments, the Senate approved the creation of a federal clearinghouse for students to shop for the best loan terms, require teacher-preparation programs to set "annual, quantifiable" goals for increasing teachers in high-demand areas such as science and mathematics, and require the Government Accountability Office (GAO) to research the possibility of gathering information on the employment of college graduates (Field 2007b).

On the House side, the House Education and the Workforce Committee took up the legislation in November of 2007, spending over two days debating some thirty amendments and approving over twenty. Among the amendments that the committee adopted would furnish grants to higher education institutions that collaborate with local employers to align the institutions' programs with labor needs, an amendment offered by Representative Jason Altmire (D-PA). The committee also approved an amendment by Congressman Robert C. Scott (D-VA) that would permit the recipients of TRIO grants to challenge the secretary of education's decision not to renew their grants. Perhaps the most controversial of the amendments that were approved took out the language from the bill that would have given colleges and universities the authority for creating measures of student learning. The Bush administration wanted to impose those measures in a centralized fashion, through the regional accreditors. The amendment, sponsored by Representative Robert E. Andrews (D-NJ), was supported by accrediting organizations but opposed by colleges and universities (Field 2007a).

In February of 2008, the House overwhelmingly approved, by a vote of 354-58, its version of the legislation, known as HR 4137. Before passing the bill, however, the House approved a rule along party lines prohibiting consideration of a number of Republican amendments "that would have prevented federal student aid from going to illegal immigrants; required colleges that use affirmation action to disclose their admissions policies; and cut off federal funds to colleges that 'partner with any entity' that discriminates against the military" (Field 2008c). The Bush administration, meanwhile, announced its opposition to this version of the bill. In a statement, the president noted that the bill would "hamper the department's ability to protect the integrity of the large federal investment in postsecondary education and to help students and parents make informed decisions about college. While college affordability is a worthy goal, the administration opposes tuition price controls or any attempt to require the justification of pricing to the U.S. government instead of consumers, who are best able to decide such issues" (qtd. in Field 2008a).

During the summer of 2008, the House and Senate versions of the legislation moved toward a compromise. The fundamental issues during this phase appear to have been college-cost watch lists (naming the most expensive and least expensive institutions and those with the highest percentage increases), the role of the Department of Education in accreditation matters, state higher education spending (with some advocating for a so-called "maintenance of effort" provision which would withhold certain federal funds from states that cut their higher education appropriations to their institutions), campus piracy, and the cost of textbooks, among others. After considerable debate and several months of discussions, the negotiators from both chambers approved the overall compromise package in July of 2008. Among the Senate conferees, the vote was 18–3; on the House side, it was 22–1 (Field 2008b).

The legislation then moved back to both chambers, where both houses approved the compromise bill. The vote on final passage was 380-49 in the House and 83-8 in the Senate (Field 2008d). In general, during floor speeches, members noted that the bill could "clean up conflicts of interest in the federal student-loan programs, make it easier for students to compare colleges on costs, simplify the process of applying for federal student aid, and generally make college more affordable" (Field 2008d). With some reluctance and somewhat unceremoniously, President Bush signed the bill into law in August of 2008. However, Margaret Spellings, the president's education secretary, voiced displeasure about many new programs in the law. While she and the administration supported many aspects of the legislation, she expressed concern about the more than 60 "'new, costly, and duplicative programs'" that the legislation created (qtd. in Hebel 2008). Those concerns, nonetheless, do not appear to have been significant enough for the president to veto the bill.

Bush administration officials spent the next several months in negotiations over rule-making, an attempt to come up with regulatory language to execute the law. In that process, the Department of Education held a half-a-dozen day-long hearings across the country in the fall of 2008 to listen to concerns from a variety of constituencies, which the department would take into account in crafting the specific regulations. The conversations centered mostly around student loans, grants, and accreditation, among others.

KEY COMPONENTS OF THE LAW

The law attempts to address a number of key issues impacting higher education. Among its main components are college costs, student financial aid, accreditation, and new reporting and disclosure requirements. The law also creates many new spending programs.

The issue of college cost has been a matter of concern for members of Congress, for students and their parents, and indeed for the general public. While the law fails to impose price controls on institutions, it imposes a variety of requirements aimed at greater transparency in an effort to restrain institutions from increasing tuition and fees at a fast pace. Indeed, in early discussions, some members of Congress proposed "withholding federal aid from students at colleges whose tuitions increased faster than consumer prices" (Hartle 2008, 10). The final bill, however, requires the Department of Education to publish annual lists (in nine institutional categories) showing the top 5 percent of institutions with the largest increases in tuition and fees and net price. The institutions on these lists are required to justify those increases and the steps underway to contain them. The Department's annual report on these institutions would be made public through the College Navigator website. This provision was designed effectively to create a "wall of shame" of institutions that increased tuition and fees at a disproportionate rate.

Additionally, the law requires the Department to post on the College Navigator website detailed information (in twenty-seven categories) about each institution that receives Title IV funds. The information includes the mission of the institution, data on applications, enrollments, transfers, degrees awarded, faculty, and a host of other items. The institutions had previously provided much of this information to the Department, but the information would now be made public, available to consumers in a searchable format.

With reference to cost, members of Congress see a clear connection between reductions in state spending on higher education and increases in tuition at public institutions. While Congress could not require states to maintain support for higher education, it created a "maintenance of effort" requirement for the states. Essentially, this requires the states to maintain a certain level of expenditure for public and private institutions. If not, the states would not be entitled to funds under a new College Access Challenge Grant Program.

The second major component of the 2008 reauthorization dealt with provisions concerning the federal financial aid to students. The law increased the maximum award for the Pell Grant Program, and made several changes in the program designed to ease eligibility (made the grant available on a year-round basis rather than just during the academic year) and set minimum awards (at 10 percent of the total annual award). The law also increased borrowing limits on federal student loans, decreased the interest charged on subsidized loans, and permitted graduates to be eligible for deferment on their PLUS loans.

Perhaps more importantly, the law sought to simplify the federal financial aid application process by streamlining the questions on the Department's Free Application for Federal Student Aid (FAFSA) form. The previous form spanned five pages, contained nearly one hundred questions, three worksheets, and had six pages of instructions. The law required the Department to create a short, two-page EZ-FAFSA specifically for low-income students, and asked the Department to shrink the number of questions of the full FAFSA by half. It also directs the Department to develop a model financial aid form that institutions could use to offer aid to students in a simplified way, and it directs the Department to create a system to allow students to get an early estimate of the amount of financial aid they might receive.

Moreover, the law contains language intended to assist veterans who left for military duty and want to return to postsecondary education. It provides a right to readmission at an institution with the same academic standing that the veteran had at last attendance, except if the veteran was discharged dishonorably or had performed bad conduct. The law also calls for the creation of a website by the Department to provide information regarding financial aid and other benefits for service members in a searchable fashion.

Accreditation was another major focus of the 2008 reauthorization law. In several ways, the law seeks to limit the Department's control over accreditors. It prohibits the Department, for example, from establishing standards that accreditors must use in judging their institutions' success regarding student achievement. The law states: "'Nothing in this section shall be construed to permit the Secretary to establish any criteria that specifies, defines, or prescribes the standards that accrediting agencies or associations shall use to assess any institution's success with respect to student achievement'" (qtd. in Hartle 2008, 11). It leaves that prerogative to institutions. The law also calls for greater transparency and due process in the accreditation processes to include making publicly available a summary of their actions, including adverse actions, and establishing an appeals body, distinct from the initial decision-making body, which has no conflict of interest in the decisions.

The law further states that accrediting bodies must respect the stated mission of the institutions, including religious missions, and can apply the same standards for evaluation of distance education that are applied for traditional teaching modalities. It also restructures the National Committee on Institutional Quality and Integrity (NACIQI), an advisory committee used by the Department to recognize accrediting agencies, by removing the appointment authority of its members solely from the Secretary to a sharing of appointments by the Secretary and members of Congress, limiting the Department's control on the committee's decision making.

Perhaps the greatest burden on institutions came in the form of many new reporting and record-keeping requirements. According to Hartle, "Taken together, the act's new mandates constitute the single biggest increase in federal regulatory burdens imposed on colleges and universities since the first Higher Education Act was passed in 1965" (2008, 11). These include matters concerning campus crime, campus emergency procedures, drug and alcohol abuse, fire safety, missing person procedures, peer-to-peer file sharing, textbooks, disaggregation of graduation data (by gender, race, ethnicity, recipients of Pell Grants and subsidized federal loans, etc.), post-graduate information, transfer of credit, voter registration, and lobbying, among others. "In some cases, the new requirements largely duplicate or substantially overlap existing statutory requirements" (Hartle 2008, 11).

Hartle concludes: "The end result, of course, is that institutions will face an enormous growth in their regulatory interactions with the Department of Education. Bales of new forms are inevitable. The chance for errors and honest mistakes grows. And, of course, administrative costs increase. It is the biggest irony of the reauthorization that a law that seeks to lower college prices includes a huge increase in the cost of doing business, a cost that will, inevitably, be passed on to consumers in the form of higher tuition" (2008, 11).

Last but not least, the act created dozens of new spending programs. They include such topics as teacher quality enhancement (e.g. Preparing Teachers for Digital Age Learners, Adjunct Teacher Corps), student assistance (Loan Forgiveness for Service in Areas of National Need, Civic Education and Participation Activities), international education (Science and Technology Advanced Foreign Language Education Grant Program), and graduate and postsecondary improvement programs (for Historically Black Colleges and Universities (HBCUs) and for students with disabilities). Additional programs include American History for Freedom, Improving College Enrollment by Secondary Schools, Grants to Create Bridges from Jobs to Careers, Grants to Rural-Serving Institutions of Higher Education, University Sustainability Programs, and many more. Almost all of these are discretionary programs, requiring appropriations from Congress. However, given the tight federal budget situation, such appropriations would be difficult. "The bottom line is that the federal government is not likely to have much money to support new programs—no matter how worthy they might be" (Hartle 2008, 13).

EVALUATION AND NEXT STEPS

As with any complex piece of legislation of recent years, the law appears to represent many compromises reflecting the interests of a variety of constituencies. As such, it is far from a coherent piece of legislation, with many provisions to the satisfaction of some groups but not everyone. For some observers, the law fell short on several counts. On the issue of student aid, for example, Baum notes that one of the key steps would be for Congress to "drastically simplify the application process and the array of student-aid programs with different eligibility requirements, regulations, and qualifying expenses. It could also do more to increase educational opportunities if it focused its subsidies on needy students who face the severest financial constraints" (2008). On aspects of accountability, Miller argues that law produced "a mishmash of new programs, new reporting requirements, and a lot of sound and fury signifying very little in the way of successful efforts to address access, affordability, or accountability" (2008).

Barmak Nassirian (2008) summarizes, in both general and particular terms, his overall sentiments regarding the legislation as follows:

> A few of the bill's provisions are perfectly sensible improvements over current law. Regrettably, however, most of this verbose legislation consists of a laundry list of bad ideas, half-thoughts, and pet peeves masquerading as deliberative federal policy . . . Like most modern legislation, many of the procedural mandates are poorly drafted and badly thought through. Those will keep Congress busy next year as it works on the inevitable technical-amendments package to clean up the most egregious of the bill's unworkable features. But the greater failure of the bill is its absence of purpose. For all its nearly 1,200-page heft and despite its 10-year gestation, it simply misses the obvious as it gets lost in legislating to yesterday's headlines . . . On important issues like college costs, program integrity, predatory private-label lending, and low-income access, the legislation offers few meaningful remedies, and on virtually all of these, it ineptly or inadvertently includes provisions that are likely to make things worse rather than better. The blame for this monumental lost opportunity falls on all the participants in the political process, not just on Congress. The administration and people in higher-education itself deserve much of the blame because they, too, have failed to develop affirmative policy proposals for Congress to act upon. In the absence of a thoughtful policy-development process, politicians are left with free hands and few tools to craft new laws as they see fit. That degeneration and surrender of public policy to the political process has predictable results: more and more laws with less and less substance.

In the end, this law was a product of political compromises and many legislative maneuvers over a period of five or more years.

Since its passage, the law has indeed achieved some of its objectives. Applying for student aid seems to be easier than before and there is more consumer information than before about costs and outcomes. On the larger goals of affordability, accountability, and transparency, however, most observers agree that the law has fallen short. While it is easier to apply for student aid and students have more information, "it's not clear that the new information is getting through to students, or that it's influencing their behavior. While surveys suggest that cost calculators are catching on, they also show that roughly half of traditional-age students still use sticker price rather than net price to make decisions about where to apply. Some colleges' calculators are difficult to find, and to use, and a lack of standardization makes cost comparisons tricky . . ." (Field 2013). On accountability, the department has published institutional "cost lists" several times to shame high-cost colleges, but tuition and fees at institutions have continued to rise. And on transparency, while many new reporting requirements on topics such as textbooks and campus crime have made more information available to the public, those same requirements have also increased the cost of doing business at institutions. For higher education generally, "the law's chief legacy may be greater federal oversight and a mountain of new reporting requirements" (Field 2013). In the end, in reference to the 2008 legislation, David Bergeron, a veteran of the Department of Education, recently said: "'It was a lot of words, and a lot of ink, but with very little accomplished. But it felt really significant at the time'" (qtd. in Field 2013).

At the time of this publication, Congress has spent several years discussing the next reauthorization of the Higher Education Act. There have been numerous hearings at committee-level, especially on the House side, with a focus on more transparent information for students and families, simplification of student aid, promotion of access and completion, and greater accountability (House Education and the Workforce Committee 2014). Many details, however, remain far from clear. In the end, two elements will ultimately override others in the reauthorization: budgetary constraints and politics. Indeed, politics and budget will likely trump policy ideas. It will take the next round of legislative process, however long that may take, for the legislation to take shape and for the details to emerge.

REFERENCES

Baum, Sandy. 2008. "The New Higher Education Act: Where It Comes Up Short." *Chronicle of Higher Education*, August 8.

Baumgartner, Frank R. and Bryan D. Jones. 1993. *Agendas and Instability in American Politics*. Chicago: University of Chicago Press.

Cobb, Roger W., and Charles D. Elder. 1983. *Participation in American Politics: The Dynamics of Agenda-Building*, 2nd ed. Baltimore: Johns Hopkins University Press.

Field, Kelly. 2007a. "House Education Committee Passes Sweeping Higher-Education Bill." *Chronicle of Higher Education*, November 2007.

Field, Kelly. 2007b. "Senate Debates Higher Education Act, Rejecting Controversial Amendment to Create Federal Loan Program." *Chronicle of Higher Education*, July 24.

Field, Kelly. 2007c. "Senate Panel Approves Bills That Would Increase Student Aid and Renew Higher Education Act." *Chronicle of Higher Education*, June 21.

Field, Kelly. 2007d. "Senate Passes Higher-Education Bill, Including Code for College-Lender Ties." *Chronicle of Higher Education*, August 3.

Field, Kelly. 2008a. "Bush Announces Opposition to Bill Renewing Higher Education Act." *Chronicle of Higher Education*, February 6.

Field, Kelly. 2008b. "House and Senate Negotiators Approve Compromise Higher Education Act." *Chronicle of Higher Education*, July 30.

Field, Kelly. 2008c. "House Passes Sweeping Bill to Renew Higher Education Act." *Chronicle of Higher Education*, February 8.

Field, Kelly. 2008d. "Long-Overdue Higher-Education Bill Is Close to Becoming Law." *Chronicle of Higher Education*, August 1.

Field, Kelly. 2013. "5 Years On, Renewed Higher-Ed Act Has Lost Its Luster." *Chronicle of Higher Education*, August 12.

Hartle, Terry W. 2008. "Coming Soon: Lots More Federal Regulations." *Trusteeship*. Association of Governing Boards of Universities and Colleges, November/December.

Hebel, Sara. 2008. "President Bush Signs Legislation to Renew the Higher Education Act." *Chronicle of Higher Education*, August 14.

House Education and the Workforce Committee. 2014. "Committee Leaders Unveil Principles for Strengthening America's Higher Education System." Press Release, June 24.

Kingdon, John W. 1995. *Agendas, Alternatives, and Public Policies*, 2nd Ed. New York: HarperCollins.

Miller, Charles. 2008. "The New Higher Education Act: Where It Comes Up Short." *Chronicle of Higher Education*, August 8.

Nassirian, Barmak. 2008. "The New Higher Education Act: Where It Comes Up Short." *Chronicle of Higher Education*, August 8.

SIX

Bipartisan Campaign Reform Act and *Citizens United v. FEC* (2002, 2010)

Peter J. Bergerson, Margaret E. Banyan, Ashley Skalecki, and Aleea L. Perry

The 2002 BPCR legislation and subsequent 2010 *Citizen's United* Supreme Court case reflects a decade-long set of legislative, executive, judicial, and interest group compromises to produce a set of campaign finance regulations. This portrait of the decision-making processes reflects a disjointed, disorderly, politically contentious, and laborious decade-long institutional struggle. The following discussion outlines this struggle in various arenas, including the evolution of campaign finance, the legislative process, the president's role, interest group influence, public opinion, court challenges, and the process of implementation. The end result of the legislation was perhaps different, but no better than conditions prior to reform.

The uneasy relationship between interest groups and the institutions of government has been a central feature of American politics from its founding. Though factions are essential to the free expression of interests and minority rights, the potential for powerful groups to dominate over other interests is significant. James Madison's *Federalist Paper No. 10* addressed the control of factions. Madison's concerns centered on achieving balance where factions though "united and activated by some common impulse of passion, or of interest, [were] adverse to the rights of other citizens, or to the permanent and aggregate interests of the community" (Madison 1787). Madison's discussion highlighted that a faction need not necessarily be a majority to have adverse effects and therefore justified some means for control. Madison argued that the most realistic control of factions was to control its effects by ensuring a representative form of government (Madison 1787). However, as elections have evolved, increasingly a representative institutional structure does not offer sufficient control. Campaign finance has become the arena in which factions exert their influence, and as a result, there has been increased interest in regulation as one of the means for their control. The Bipartisan Campaign Reform Act (BCRA) of 2002 was one such attempt to regulate campaign finance. However, as the legislation was implemented, the regulation of campaign finance has become increasingly bureaucratic and court challenges have essentially increased opportunities for interest group influence over elections.

EVOLUTION OF REGULATION AND CAMPAIGN FINANCE REFORM

Factions, or interest groups, in the United States expanded rapidly in the late 1960s and early 1970s, many of which represented citizens and their social concerns (Interest Group System 2010). In response to this growth, there was a growing need to regulate their negative effects. This is consistent with the generally accepted notion that regulation of the private market is a way to correct the "various defects or failures in the open, or free, marketplace" (Warren 2011, 75). Government regulation also functions to control the narrow interests of factions. Generally, attitudes toward government regulation have evolved toward a "pro-governmental regulation" point of view. However, both proponents for and against government regulation of campaign finance are active in the BCRA lawmaking process. Supporters of regulation believe that it offers advantages for democratic accountability by requiring the government to act fairly in the execution of its tasks. Supporters also believe that regulation protects individuals from each other by requiring open access to information to prevent "excessive and counterproductive competition" (Warren 2011, 80). On the other hand, opponents of government regulation believe that regulations are oppressive and are likely to serve only the interests of the most powerful groups. In the opponents' opinion, the best way to achieve the interests of society is to allow the free market to create natural limits on behavior (Warren 2011). However, when the private marketplace conflicts with the election of representatives, it leads to concerns over fairness and faction.

Regulation of campaign finance as a way to control factions mostly developed within the last century. In 1907, President Theodore Roosevelt spoke out against campaign corruption, which was followed by the Tillman Act that outlawed contributions by private corporations to federal congressional and presidential elections. This was followed by the Federal Corruption Practices Act of 1925 that attempted to establish public disclosure rules. Later in the 1940s, the Tillman Act and the Taft-Hartley Act were used to place dollar limits on contributions and labor union contributions. Labor unions responded by creating political action committees (PACs), a move that was quickly followed by businesses. The 1970s birthed the modern campaign finance rules that evolved from the Federal Election Campaign Act (FECA). The FECA set contribution limits, required disclosure of contributions from individual donations of $200 or more, and created the Federal Election Commission (FEC) to carry out the provisions of the bill ("A Century of U.S. Campaign Finance Law" 2010). Individual donations were limited to $1,000 per candidate per election in 1974. The 1976 landmark Supreme Court case *Buckley v. Valeo* tested the constitutionality of the FECA and concluded that individuals had the right to exercise their free speech by spending, but not contributing, unlimited political money. Regulations continued to be tested throughout the 1980s and 1990s as the "soft money" loophole was exploited. Soft money is typically considered money that is not directed toward a particular candidate, but may go to fund the party instead. While contributions to individual candidate campaigns were limited, the amount that corporations, unions, and individuals gave to national parties for "party building activities" was not. The use of soft money was significant in the 1996 election year (Grant 1998).

Improper fundraising scandals such as the Jack Abramoff saga led to the public outcry for a "second-wave" of reform and put campaign finance at the top of the political agenda. The subsequent reform attempt came in the form of the Bipartisan Campaign Reform Act of 2002, sponsored by Senators John McCain (R-AZ) and Russ Feingold (D-WI). Michael Malbin (2006) summarized the BCRA as follows:

> The main provisions in BCRA prohibited unlimited soft money contributions to national political parties for any purpose and to state parties for 'federal election activity.' The law also prohibited corporate or labor union funding of certain 'electioneering' ads and required disclosure of individual financing for electioneering. BCRA is best understood as an attempt to patch and repair the older system because it had sprung major leaks. Specifically, BCRA is an attempt to restore meaningful contribution limits and disclosure to federal campaign finance law. (Malbin 2006, 4–5)

The BCRA defines electioneering ads as those ads that are "(1) conveyed by a broadcast, cable, or satellite communication; (2) broadcast to a market of at least 50,000 people in the relevant electorate; (3) names or identifies a federal candidate; and (4) airs within sixty days of a general election or thirty days of a primary" (Malbin 2006, 7). At the same time, individual contribution limits were also increased under BCRA from $1,000 to $2,000 per election (Malbin 2006).

INSTITUTIONAL ACTORS AND THE LEGISLATIVE PROCESS

Passage of the BCRA was primarily action taken through the U.S. House of Representatives with relatively little public attention. The usual suspects of elected officials, interest groups, and bureaucratic agencies were involved. The following describes the BCRA legislative process involving major institutional actors including, the Congressional Research Service, House of Representatives, and participation of the Congressional Budget Office.

Congressional Research Service

An indispensable agency in the legislative process is the Congressional Research Service (CRS). This agency is a unit of the Library of Congress and assists members of the U.S. House and Senate throughout the legislative process, including drafting of a bill, detailed research, the committee debate and discussion, floor action, and implementation. The outputs of the CRS staff include the "who," "what," "why," "when," and "how" of legislation by producing reports on major policy issues, confidential memoranda, briefings and consultations, seminars and workshops. The CRS uses expert congressional testimony and responses to individual inquiries.

The CRS report on the BCRA provided the step-by-step process of how the enactment of McCain-Feingold would work. Essentially, it resembled the labyrinth of the Greek tunnel system. Because of the complex and historic nature of the legislation, five standing committees and four subcommittees worked on the bill before it reached the floor of the House. These included the House Administration Committee, the House Education and the Workforce Committee (including the Subcommittee on House Education and the Workforce Subcommittee on Employer-Employee Relations), the House Government Reform Committee (including the Subcommittee on House Government Reform and the Subcommittee on Government Efficiency, Financial Management and Intergovernmental Relations), the House Judiciary Committee, the House Ways and Means Committee, and the House Rules Committee.

U.S. House of Representatives

Committees assigned to the BCRA in 2002 filed two reports. In the House, Report 107-131 was filed by Rep. Ney of the Committee on House Administration and Report 107-135 was filed by Rep. Reynolds of the Committee on Rules (House Report No. 107-31, Pt.1, 2001; House Report No. 107-35, 2001).

Report 107-131 of the House Administration Committee showed that five separate hearings on BCRA were held between March 2001 and June

2001. One of the hearings was a "field hearing"—that is, a hearing that was held outside Washington, DC. In this case, the hearing was held in Phoenix, AZ. Arizona is represented by one of the Senate co-sponsors, Sen. McCain. The remaining four hearings were held in Washington, D.C. with a diverse set of witnesses that included interest groups, elected officials, and bureaucrats. Witnesses also included labor, business, and ideological interest groups. These included representatives from the Arizona Civil Liberties Union, the Arizona League of Women Voters, the Arizona Good Government Association, the Arizona Restaurant Association, and the AFL-CIO. State and federal elected officials also participated in the hearings, including representation from the Arizona state legislature, and three of four congressional sponsors (Rep. Gephardt, Rep. DeLay, Rep. Shays, Rep. Meehan, Sen. Hagel, Sen. McConnell and Sen. Feingold) (House Report No. 107-31, Pt.1, 2001). The bureaucracy was also represented through the participation of the Federal Election Commission.

Although the House Administration Committee ultimately filed an adverse report on the BCRA, three members of the committee, Representatives Steny Hoyer, Chaka Fattah, and Jim Davis noted in their minority views that the bill was essential to campaign finance reform (House Report No. 107-31, Pt.1, 2001). Part of the legislative process required consideration of the budget using information provided by the Congressional Budget Office.

Congressional Budget Office

In the early 1990s, budget reform legislation required a "Pay-as-You-go Estimate" to be provided by the Congressional Budget Office (CBO) to members of Congress before a bill could become a law. The "soft money" provision of BCRA for national political parties includes both civil and criminal fines for violation of the 2002 law. Civil fines, if collected under the statute, would be classified as government revenue and thus subject to CBO estimate. In the 2002 CBO report to Congress, it estimated that any fines would "not be significant" but that if there were fines they would be considered criminal fines and be deposited in the "Crime Victims Fund" (Congressional Budget Office 2002).

As a result of the CRS Report, House committees and subcommittees, and the CBO, the House Rules Committee recommended that the BCRA be adopted—in other words, be put up to a vote as early as June 12, 2001 (House Report No. 107-35, 2001). The legislation passed the House on February 14, 2002, by a vote of 240–189 and was sent on to the Senate. The Senate by-passed the committee stage and voted on the bill as passed by the House. On March 3, 2002, the Senate invoked a cloture vote on the legislation by a vote of 68–32 to end debate and discussion. The Senate approved the legislation sponsored by McCain and Feingold.

The President's Role

President Bush had important influence over the process as well. Bush took a laissez faire attitude toward the BCRA. In his 2000 presidential campaign, he raised concerns about the constitutionality of the legislation. Shortly before the legislation was enacted, in a letter to then Senate Majority Leader Trent Lott (R-MS), the president outlined his priorities, including (1) strengthening the role of individuals in the political process; (2) maintaining strong political parties; (3) eliminating involuntary contributions; (4) banning corporate and union soft money; and (5) disclosing contributions and expenditures in a way that was full, open, prompt, and constitutional. Bush was particularly concerned about union campaign contributions, arguing that no one should be forced to support a candidate or cause against his or her will. Anticipating a possible court challenge, Bush favored a non-severability provision that provided that if any part of the bill was found unconstitutional, the Supreme Court would void the entire bill. In the end, President Bush signed the bill into law on March 27, 2002, indicating that although the legislation was "far from perfect," it "represents progress" and "will improve current financing campaigns for federal campaigns" (Woolley and Peters 2013).

Interest Groups

As highlighted in the introduction, the national debate by special interest groups surrounding the BCRA reflected the early insights of Madison in *The Federalist No. 10*. Madison warned readers of the "instability, injustice, and confusion introduced into the public councils" by what he labeled "factions," or what we would call today as special interest groups (Madison 1787).

As might be expected with such a sweeping bill, a wide range of social, economic, and political interest groups produced a cascade of opinions about PACS, constitutional rights, and the role of interest groups in campaigns (Boatright 2011). Two broad categories of interest groups, access and ideologically-oriented organizations, were affected by the BCRA and actively expressed their views (Boatright 2011).

Access-oriented groups are concerned with assuring continued access to lawmakers that shape public policy. These and other groups seek to preserve their option to influence specific policy issues and determine who will get what, when, and how. They most often provide contributions to incumbents or those who are safe bets to win an election. Examples of access-oriented groups include associations such as Trial Lawyers of America and the National Association of Realtors. Those seeking access to elected officials make contributions based on requests from candidates, campaign bundlers, or financial managers and label this money as being "pulled" into the campaign (Boatright 2011).

Ideologically-oriented groups are those who focus on influencing who is elected in order to preserve their policy position. These include groups such as the National Rifle Association and the Sierra Club. They tend to take an active role in the nominating process, primary elections, and general elections. Distinct from other types of contributions, ideologically-oriented groups "push" contributions into the political process to determine who wins the election (Malbin, Rozell, and Wilcox 2003).

The impact of BCRA on interest groups is tentative because once FEC establishes rules and regulations, campaign professionals tend to find "loopholes" which alter the campaign landscape. A summary of conclusions from campaign observers have suggested several outcomes of BCRA, including that existing PACs have been strengthened, access and ideologically-oriented groups have developed new PACs, fundraising has began earlier than in the past, access groups have begun to bundle more money, the balance of power within interest groups has been altered, and there has been an increase in 527 ideological groups (Herrnson 2005). The combined result is that there has been an increase in fundraising that favors incumbents and large contributions. This has altered the role of political parties as an organizing entity as campaigns are increasingly about the candidate and not their platform.

Public Opinion and BCRA

The public policy process in the twenty-first century has seen the ubiquitous presence of and debate over the merits of public opinion polling. A wide range of media groups, public advocacy groups, and supporters as well as opponents of policy issues often use polling to legitimatize their position on national issues. This was the case with the BCRA. National organizations such as the *New York Times*, the *Washington Post*, *ABC News*, Pew Research, Gallup, and Rasmussen all reported polls on campaign financing (Eilperin and Clement 2013; Ergun 2012; Moore 2001; Rasmussen Reports 2012; "Why Americans Aren't Stirred by Campaign Finance Reform" 2001). Over an extended period of time, a wide variety of polls reported significant public support for restrictions on campaign contributions. The public mood did not correspond to the respondent's self-identified party's position. For example, a March 2008 Gallup poll found that Democrats (whose party has generally supported spending limits) opposed them by 54 percent to 42 percent. Republicans (whose party has generally opposed spending limits) favor them by 64 percent to 33 percent (Jones 2008). Further, public support for regulating legislation is clearly a bipartisan issue. In January 2012, Rasmussen polls reported that 58 percent of adults, regardless of political affiliation, think the country needs more campaign finance laws (Rasmussen Reports 2012).

Still, even though respondents articulated their position on the issue, generally the polling showed that the public is skeptical at best about campaign finance reform legislation. A March 2002 Gallup poll found that that 67 percent of adults felt special interests will maintain power as the U.S. Senate battled over the McCain-Feingold bill (Jones 2002).

More significant is that Super PACs have created the appearance of corruption and seriously undermined public confidence in elections and democracy. Polls have demonstrated that a significant majority of the public is opposed to Super PACS. In a March 2012 *Washington Post-ABC News* poll, nearly seven in ten Americans—69 percent—said Super PACs should be illegal (Ergun 2012). Further, 67 percent of both the major parties believe that there should be legal limits on how much independent groups can spend on campaigns (Eilperin and Clement 2013). Other polls confirmed this public position. For example, in June of 2013, a Gallup poll found that 79 percent of those polled would vote for a law that would limit the amount of money candidates for the U.S. House and Senate could spend on their campaigns for election ("Politics," 2013).

Perhaps the most serious implication of these polls is that a fundamental ideal of the U.S. electoral process has been eroded in two ways. First, public confidence that elections are an open, fair, and transparent process is a keystone element of our political system. The public's perception of huge sums of unaccounted dollars for contributions, the unknown role of Super PACs, and unlimited independent expenditures on political advertisements have led to the appearance of corruption and an erosion of confidence in elections and public officials. Justice John Paul Stevens, in his dissenting opinion in *Citizens United*, best reflected the opinion of the public when he wrote that "the Court's opinion is thus a rejection of the common sense of the American people, who have recognized a need to prevent corporations from undermining self-government since the founding, and who have fought against the distinctive corrupting potential of corporate electioneering since the days of Theodore Roosevelt" (*Citizens United v. FEC* 2010).

Second, the polls suggest that a new challenge for the public has been introduced into political campaigns. Today, an informed voting public must now master a glossary of modern era vocabulary terms associated with campaign finance. Federal, state, and local campaign finance legislation, FEC rules, and political party funding practices have produced a subculture with its own political dialect. In addition to the routine of campaigns such as candidates' policy positions, debates, and campaign commercials, the public must now grasp the significance of terms such as "super PACs," "soft money," "unnamed sources," and "coordinated campaigns."

CITIZENS UNITED AND THE BCRA

After passage of the BCRA, several court cases affected the goal of the legislation to curb interest group influence on campaigns. In 2003, *McConnell v. the Federal Election Commission* was the first major case brought to the United States Supreme Court against the BCRA. The main arguments of the plaintiffs in *McConnell* were that the "soft money" ban of the BCRA exceeded Congress' authority to regulate elections under Article 1, Section 4 of the United States Constitution (allowing state legislatures to prescribe their state senators), as well as violated the First Amendment's protection of free speech. Plaintiffs argued that the regulation of political advertisements also violated the First Amendment's free speech clause (*McConnell v. FEC* 2003). The Supreme Court's majority opinion held that the regulation of contribution limits is legitimate and important because it allows the government to prevent not only actual corruption, but also the appearance of corruption. Avoiding the appearance of corruption was important for sustaining the public's confidence in the electoral process. Secondly, the Court found that Congress did not overstep its authority because the BCRA only affected state elections that federal candidates were involved in; states were still able to create their own laws for elections at state and local levels. Lastly, the Court upheld a precedent (*Austin v. Michigan Chamber of Commerce*) stating that political speech by corporations may be regulated because their opinions can unfairly influence elections (*McConnell v. FEC* 2003). This decision would be the standard for seven years.

While the *McConnell* case mostly upheld the constitutionality of the BCRA, Citizens United once again challenged its provisions in 2010. Citizens United is a nonprofit organization that is better known for its politically motivated feature film "Hillary: The Movie." The goal was to air the movie on video-on-demand cable television within 30 days of the primary election. To acquire viewers, the group produced television ads for the program's feature. Citizens United was denied injunctive relief against the BCRA by a federal district court and the movie was prohibited from being shown before the 2008 election. It proceeded to appeal to the Supreme Court. This set the stage for a challenge to the constitutionality of the BCRA with the following arguments: that the BCRA's ban on corporations and labor unions using general funds to create electioneering ads was unconstitutional, and that the BCRA's disclaimer and disclosure requirements were unconstitutional as applied to *Hillary* and the ads (*Citizens United v. FEC* 2010). The decisions made in *Citizens United* are especially important because the Court overturned several of its previous decisions as well as fundamentally voided part of the BCRA. The Court decided that there was no basis for the government to limit independent corporate expenditures because they recognized that the First Amendment protects corporations. It also decided that since "speech is an essential mechanism of democracy—it is the means to hold officials accountable to the people—political speech must prevail against laws that would suppress it" (*Citizens United v. FEC* 2010); essentially that there is no sufficient government interest to justify the contrary.

Where in *McConnell* the Court allowed speech to be banned based on corporate identity; after *Citizens*, this was no longer the case. Still, the Court upheld the *McConnell* precedent regarding disclosure rules by stating that advertisements fall within the legislation's definition of "electioneering communication" and that "disclosure can be justified by a governmental interest in providing the electorate with information about election-related spending sources" (*Citizens United v. FEC* 2010). The decisions made by the Court in the *Citizens United* case had important implications for the BCRA. The use of "soft money" played a big role in the participation of corporations and appearance of corruption within the federal election process, especially during the 1996 presidential election, which is the main reason that the BCRA was created. The case essentially overturned this provision, allowing for corporations and labor unions to contribute limitless funds to PACs once again (*Citizens United v. FEC* 2010).

THE OUTCOMES: IMPLEMENTING THE BCRA

In the wake of the *Citizens United* decision, the president and legislators interested in campaign finance once again spoke to the nation about the need for reform. As the legislation evolved and the process of implementation began, the executive branch attempted to influence the more negative aspects of the court challenge. This highlighted the role of the president and the Federal Elections Commission.

President Barack Obama

President Obama was a passionate and ardent supporter of the BCRA and an outspoken critic of its opponents. On three different occasions, Obama addressed the campaign finance issue, the Supreme Court's ruling, and congressional action. Two days following the Supreme Court's decision, in a weekly radio address, he argued that "even foreign corporations may now get into the act" of spending "an unlimited amount of special interest money" for political purposes. Later that month, in his January 27, 2010, State of the Union Address, President Obama took the highly unusual approach to publicly criticize the Supreme Court's 5–4 decision in *Citizens United v. Federal Election Commission* in striking down the landmark legislation. The president told the joint session that "last week the Supreme Court reversed a century of law that I believe will open the floodgates for special interests; to spend without limit in our elections." He went on in his address to call on "Democrats and Republicans to pass a bill that helps to right this wrong" (Jacobson 2010).

In July 2010, President Obama addressed the issue a third time at a Rose Garden press conference. The president outlined what the court decision will mean to congressional campaigns. He suggested that now "new limitless flows of undisclosed money" will encourage "shadow groups," conceal contributors, and result in an "onslaught of negative ads" (Lee 2010). He lamented that now special interests such as "corporate lobbyists" will have "war chests" of tens of millions of dollars to determine the outcome of congressional elections. The president used the Rose Garden event to call on the U.S. Senate to pass the DISCLOSE Act which would simply require corporate political advertisers to reveal who's funding their activities and open campaigns contributions to more transparency (Lee 2010). The DISCLOSE Act passed in the 111th House, but failed in the Senate.

The Federal Election Commission

The role of the FEC was also critical to the evolution of the BCRA. However, as the legislation evolved, its role has become increasingly bureaucratized and the FEC now largely functions as a bookkeeper rather than providing essential policy oversight. Congress established the FEC in 1975 as an administrative agency empowered to develop campaign regulations and enforce federal election laws. The responsibility of the Commission, a six-member independent regulatory agency, includes oversight of campaigning financing and monitoring statutes such as the 2002 BCRA. The FEC is charged with the authority to "disclose campaign finance information; enforce the provisions of the law such as the limits and prohibitions on contributions, and to oversee the public funding of Presidential elections." The composition of the commission was designed to produce "nonpartisan decisions." The chairmanship rotates among the members each year, with no member serving more than once during his or her term. The enabling legislation states that no more than three commissioners can be of the same party and official policy requires four affirmative votes. Each commissioner is appointed by the president, confirmed by the Senate, and serves for a six-year term ("About the FEC"). The FEC implemented the McCain-Feingold legislation by establishing definitions and rules for major provisions of the BCRA, including soft money, electioneering and independent expenditures, contribution limitations and prohibitions, disclaimers, personal use of campaign funds, and millionaire candidates. The FEC defines soft money as financial contributions outside of the limits of the federal campaign finance law. Commonly referred to as "soft money" or non-federal money, the Commission prohibits national parties from raising or spending money in federal campaigns and elections (Federal Election Commission 2002).

The legislation makes state and local parties obligated to fund certain campaign activities. The BCRA and FEC regulations also address "electioneering communications," or what is commonly referred to as "issue ads" on radio and television, but not the internet, newspapers, or telephone. "Issue ads" typically discuss candidates in the context of certain issues without specifically advocating a candidate's election or defeat. FEC rules prohibit corporations or unions from funding these commercials thirty days before a primary election and sixty days before a general election (Federal Election Commission 2002).

The legislation and FEC established a three-part test that governs "coordinated communication" among a candidate, his or her committee, and a person or group that has made a financial contribution. The three-part test includes: (1) the source of the payment, (2) if the content of the ad is related to the election, and (3) the conduct of the individual or group making the payment. In addition, the BCRA allows for an increase on the limits on contributions made by individuals and some political committees. Also, the legislation prohibits contributions and expenditures by foreign nationals (Federal Election Commission 2002).

The FEC also regulates disclaimers and personal use of campaign funds. For example, the 2002 law stipulates that campaign literature and ads must include a disclaimer of support for one candidate, that the candidate's authorized radio and television ads must include an audio statement by the candidate approving the advertisement, and that radio or television ads that are not authorized by a candidate require a written disclaimer and contact information for the sponsoring organization. Further, personal campaign funds are regulated in that while they allow congressional candidates to receive a salary from their organization and contributions may be used for certain non-campaign purposes, documentation is required for campaign expenses (Federal Election Commission 2002).

Finally, the FEC is responsible for regulating the McCain-Feingold provision that increased contribution limits for candidates facing opponents who put substantial sums of their personal funds into their own campaigns. For the House campaigns, there is a $350,000 threshold that triggers the millionaires' amendment. The expenditure ceiling in Senate elections depends on the state's population but can range from over two million dollars in California to a half-a-million in Connecticut. Once a candidate's personal contributions trips the spending threshold, he or she must notify opponents and the FEC (Federal Election Commission 2007).

CONCLUSION: ASSESSING THE BCRA

An important phase of the legislative process is an examination of the legacy left by sweeping reform measures. Recent well-intended attempts to reform campaign finance began in 1995, was enacted into law in 2002, and challenged in 2010. A decade following the implementation of the BCRA provides the opportunity to reflect and assess on its four critical goals to (1) ban unregulated "soft money" contributions that may have undue interest group influence, (2) reduce the amount of money spent on political campaigns, (3) increase transparency in reporting, and (4) renew faith in the electoral process. While the 2002 legislation established some ground rules for campaign financing, the *Citizens United* decision quickly dashed any expectations the sponsors had of limiting the influence and amount of money spent on campaigns and elections. The impact of the Court's decision is reflected in election expenditures. One study reported that in 2012, candidates running for the U.S. Senate seats spent $587 million, twice what they did a decade earlier in 2002. In the House, members running for a seat in 2012 spent more than $923 million. The research shows that congressional incumbents who won with less than 60 percent of the vote spent an average of $2.25 million in 2012; while incumbents who lost their reelection bid spent an average of $3.1 million. A non-incumbent candidate spent an average of $1.52 million in an attempt to get elected in the 2012 congressional campaign (Ornstein, Mann, Malbin, and Rugg 2013). A poignant example of the influence on campaign spending is reflected in two non-competitive House races in 2012. Rep. Sam Johnson (R-TX) spent $972,000, while Rep. Frederica Wilson (D-FL) spent $554,000; both received 100 percent of the vote. In the 2012 elections, spending on races spiked, topping out at a total of $3.25 billion in financing (Wilson 2013).

The *Citizens United* decision also opened the door to corporations, unions, and nonprofit organizations to make contributions in federal election campaigns. Under this decision, PACs and Super PACs can raise and spend unlimited amounts of money. Further, new to the campaign finance arena are 501(c)(4) groups, legally referenced as "social welfare organizations," which can conceal their donors' identities (Matthews 2013).

The influence of factions on campaign financing is not showing any sign of slowing. The Center for Responsive Politics reported as of August 2012 that there were already 818 Super PACs registered with the FEC who had raised $23,149,887 and spent $12,024,478 in preparation for the 2014 election cycle (Center for Responsive Politics 2013).

The BCRA, at best, presented a pause and redirection of the electoral process that served merely to increase bureaucracy without any real effect on campaign financing. While it has increased the FEC's role to that of a bookkeeper, it has tended to centralize campaign contributions, nationalize candidate recruitment, increase the cost of political campaigns, and distance candidates from local citizen's accountability. Most concerning is that it has negatively impacted public confidence in the electoral process and altered the focus of "representation." The complete picture presented by the BCRA legislation and implementation alerts one to the clarion call expressed by Madison in *Federalist No. 10* when he argued that of the many advantages of the newly proposed Federal Constitution, "none deserves to be more accurately developed than its tendency to break and control the violence of faction" (Madison 1787). This, however, is an ideal that has yet to be developed in the context of modern election financing.

REFERENCES

"A Century of U.S. Campaign Finance Law." 2010. Accessed September 3, 2013. http://www.npr.org.

"About the FEC." Accessed September 3, 2013. http://www.fec.gov/about.html.

Boatright, Robert G. 2011. *Interest Groups and Campaign Finance Reform in the United States and Canada*. Ann Arbor, MI: University of Michigan Press.

Center for Responsive Politics. 2013."2014 Outside Spending, by Super PAC." Accessed September 3, 2013. http://www.opensecrets.org.

Citizens United v. Federal Election Commission. 2010. 558 U.S. 310.

Congressional Budget Office. 2002. H.R. 2356 Bipartisan Campaign Reform Act of 2002. United States Government.

Eilperin, Juliet, and Scott Clement. 2013. "Why Don't Americans Care More About Campaign Finance Reform?" *Washington Post*.

Ergun, Damla. 2012. "Seven in 10 Would Send Super PACs Packing." Accessed September 3, 2013. http://www.abcnews.com.

Federal Election Commission. 2002. "Major Provisions of the Bipartisan Campaign Reform Act." Accessed September 3, 2013. http://www.fec.gov.

Federal Election Commission. 2007. "Millionaire's Amendment: A Primer." Accessed September 3, 2013. http://www/fec.gov.

Grant, Andrew. 1998. "The Politics of American Campaign Finance." *Parliamentary Affairs* 51: 223-50.

Herrnson, Paul S. 2005. "The Bipartisan Campaign Reform Act and Congressional Elections." In *Congress Reconsidered*, 8th ed., edited by Lawrence C. Dodd and Bruce I. Oppenheimer, 107–35. Thousand Oaks, CA: Congressional Quarterly.

House Report, No. 107-31, Pt.1. 2001. Accessed September 3, 2013. http://www.gpo.gov.

House Report, No. 107-35. 2001. Accessed September 3, 2013. http://www.gpo.gov.

Interest Group System, 1976 to Present. 2010. Washington, D.C.: Congressional Quarterly.

Jacobson, Louis. 2010. "Why Alito Shook His Head: Obama Exaggerates Impact of Supreme Court Ruling on Foreign Companies." Accessed September 3, 2013. http://www.politifact.com.

Jones, Jeffrey M. 2002. "Seven in 10 Support New Campaign Finance Legislation." Accessed September 3, 2013. http://www.gallup.com.

Jones, Jeffrey M. 2008. "Campaign Finance Appears to be Non-Issue for Voters." Accessed September 3, 2013. http://www.gallup.com.

Lee, Jesse. 2010. "President Obama on Citizens United." The White House Blog. Accessed September 3, 2013. http://www.whitehouse.gov/blog.

Madison, James. 1787. *The Federalist Papers*. New York: Penguin.

Malbin, Michael J. 2006. "Assessing the Bipartisan Campaign Reform Act." In *The Election After Reform: Money, Politics, and the Bipartisan Campaign Reform Act*, 1-16. Washington, D.C.: Campaign Finance Institute.

Malbin, Michael J., Mark J. Rozell, and Clyde Wilcox. 2003. "BCRA's Impact on Interest Groups and Advocacy Organizations." In *Life After Reform: When the Bipartisan*

Campaign Reform Act Meets Politics, edited by Michael J. Malbin, 43–60. Lanham, MD: Rowman and Littlefield.

Matthews, Dylan. 2013. "Crossroads GPS and Priorities USA Were Created for the Purpose of Hiding Donors." *Washington Post*.

McConnell v. Federal Election Commission. 2003. 540 U.S. 93.

Moore, David W. 2001. "Widespread Public Support for Campaign Finance Reform." Accessed September 3, 2013. http://www.gallup.com.

Ornstein, Norman J., Thomas E. Mann, Michael J. Malbin, and Andrew Rugg. 2013. *Campaign Finance in Congressional Elections*. Washington, D.C.: Campaign Finance Institute.

"Politics." 2013. Accessed September 3, 2013. www.pollingreport.com/politics.htm.

Rasmussen Reports. 2012. "58% Say U.S. Needs New Campaign Finance Laws." Accessed September 3, 2013. http://www.rasmussenreports.com.

Warren, Kenneth F. 2011. *Administrative Law in the Political System*. 5th Edition. Boulder, CO: Westview.

"Why Americans Aren't Stirred by Campaign Finance Reform." 2001. *Pew Research Center*. Accessed September 3, 2013. http://www.people-press.org.

Wilson, Reid. 2013. "A Decade After McCain-Feingold, Election Spending Spikes." *National Journal Group*. Accessed September 3, 2013. http://www.nationaljournal.com.

Woolley, John, and Gerhard Peters. 2013. "George W. Bush XLIII President of the United States: 2001-2010 Statement on Signing the Bipartisan Campaign Reform Act of 2002." Accessed September 3, 2013. http://www.presidency.ucsb.edu.

SEVEN

Dodd-Frank Wall Street Reform and Consumer Protection Act (2010)

Marcia L. Godwin with Shandra L. McDonald

The Dodd-Frank Act (Public Law 111-203, 124 Stat. 1376) was the last of three high-profile laws to be enacted within two years of the financial crisis and the related Great Recession that began in 2008. Unlike the Troubled Asset Relief Program (TARP) and American Recovery and Reinvestment Act (ARRA), Dodd-Frank was explicitly intended as a permanent, comprehensive reform of the nation's financial system. At 2,319 pages and sixteen titles, Dodd-Frank was the longest piece of legislation in the nation's history. Most of its provisions are largely unknown to the general public, but the creation of a new government agency, the Consumer Financial Protection Bureau (CFPB), has been a lightning rod for continued controversy and public scrutiny.

This chapter examines the passage of Dodd-Frank and its implementation. As shown in table 7.1, the passage appeared to be an increasingly rare example that followed a textbook legislative process. However, there were enough exceptions along the way that it can still be dubbed "unorthodox lawmaking," to use the term coined by Barbara Sinclair (2012). Furthermore, the history of Dodd-Frank serves as an illustrative case of living legislation (Jenkins and Patashnik 2012). Increasingly, congressional scholars recognize that the adoption of legislation is not a single instance of the passage of a bill, but that policies and programs must be rejustified and amended time after time (Patashnik 2008; Jenkins and Patashnik 2012).

LEGISLATIVE PROBLEM SOLVING AND THE GREAT RECESSION

The impetus for Dodd-Frank was clearly the financial crisis that started with the bailout of investment firm Bear Sterns in March 2008 and escalated with the bankruptcy of Lehman Brothers and the collapse of insu-

Table 7.1. Chronology of Major Activities Leading to the Adoption of Dodd-Frank

Date	Activity
	2008
February	Congress approves stimulus bill as economy weakens
March	Bear Stearns bailout; deal made to be acquired by JPMorgan Chase
September	Lehman Brothers files for bankruptcy
October	Congress approves Emergency Economic Stabilization Act of 2008, establishing Troubled Asset Relief Program (TARP)
	2009
February	Congress approves American Recovery and Reinvestment Act of 2009
March	Department of Treasury issues framework for financial reform
June	Obama administration forwards draft financial reform legislation to Congress
December	House approves financial reform legislation
	2010
January	Senator Christopher Dodd (D-CT), chairman of the Senate Banking Committee, announces retirement at end of year; Scott Brown (R-MA) wins special election to Senate after Ted Kennedy's death; Obama administration announces support for Volcker Rule
April	Securities and Exchange Commission votes 3–2 to sue Goldman Sachs
May	U.S. Senate approves financial reform legislation
June 29	Conference committee meeting to reconcile House and Senate bills; legislation renamed Dodd-Frank
June 30	House approves Dodd-Frank, 237–192
July 15	Senate approves Dodd-Frank, 60–39
July 21	Dodd-Frank signed by President Obama

Source: Compiled by authors.

rance company AIG in September 2008. The crisis occurred in the midst of the fall presidential election campaign between Democrat Barack Obama and Republican John McCain. Congress was among many governmental institutions that the public blamed for failing to foresee problems with subprime housing mortgages and creative financial instruments that passed along risks to vulnerable companies, leading to the Great Recession. Congress eventually engaged in problem solving because of growing public concern, and partially made up for earlier inaction. It is important to recognize that Congress as an institution is not exclusively driven by partisan gamesmanship and responses to special interests, especially when faced with a clear crisis or problem (Mayhew 2006, 223–24; Adler and Wilkerson 2012).

The prospects for successful adoption of problem-solving legislation are enhanced when issues are visible and guided through Congress by experienced members who are skilled at creating bipartisan support (Mayhew 2006, 224–30). With both Democratic and Republican leadership support, an economic stimulus bill passed both houses of Congress within a month of being proposed in early 2008. The passage of the American Recovery and Reinvestment Act (ARRA) followed a similar route to approval a year later, albeit with more congressional committee involvement and more partisan voting patterns (Sinclair 2012, 166-85).

The adoption of the Credit Cardholder Accountability Responsibility and Disclosure Act of 2009 (H.R. 627) is an especially pertinent example of how the financial meltdown shifted partisan gridlock in favor of bipartisan action. Officially an amendment to the Truth in Lending Act, an earlier version of the proposal had stalled in Congress in 2008 but was resurrected in 2009 by Representative Carolyn Mahoney (D-NY). It easily cleared the House of Representatives at the end of April 2009 by a 357–70 vote, passed the Senate by an even wider margin of 90–5 on May 19, had a final vote in the House the next day, and was signed into law by President Obama on May 22. Some partisanship crept into the legislative process along the way, but not enough to slow down passage. It narrowly passed the Senate Banking Committee and the final House vote had more Republican opposition than the previous vote in April. There also was an unrelated addition to the Senate version (allowing visitors to bring guns into national parks) that had to be separated out for a separate vote when considered by the House (McCarty, Poole, and Rosenthal 2013, 207). Still, the swift approval and lack of effective financial industry opposition signaled that more ambitious reforms would have excellent chances of being approved as well (Kaiser 2013, 82–3; Library of Congress n.d.).[1]

The bill (H.R. 4173) that became Dodd-Frank was introduced during this chaotic time and was intended to solve two pressing concerns: (1) the need for a comprehensive update and overhaul of financial regulations, and (2) a mostly political imperative to demonstrate that Congress was sympathetic to the average citizen more than the large financial companies that triggered the Great Recession. Thus, Dodd-Frank encompassed solutions to two different types of problems, a long-standing need for reform and a more immediate crisis. A policy window opened that allowed Representative Barney Frank (D-MA) to move forward with financial reform. The establishment of a new consumer financial protection agency dealt with the new problem; adding a new agency is a typical legislative response to a perceived crisis (Kamarck 2013, 34).

THE LEGISLATIVE APPROVAL PROCESS

The approval process for major congressional legislation is well-documented through official government records and media coverage. There is even more detailed analysis available on Dodd-Frank because veteran journalist Robert Kaiser anticipated in late 2008 that landmark financial reform legislation would be passed. Kaiser decided to write a book on Dodd-Frank to illustrate legislative policymaking; it was published a few years later as *Act of Congress* (2013). Kaiser had exceptional access to Representative Frank, the chair of the House Financial Services Committee, and good rapport with legislators and staff in both houses of Congress.

Kaiser compiled a list of fifty-six participants in the legislative process: eighteen from the House of Representatives (eleven representatives, seven staff), twenty-four from the Senate (twelve senators, twelve staff), six from the executive branch, and eight from outside government (interest group representatives, economists, and reform advocates). Since there was unified Democratic government during the 111th Congress (2009-10), only six of the twenty-three legislators cited were Republicans. While then House Minority Leader John Boehner (R-OH) received passing mention in the book, it is notable that he didn't make it onto Kaiser's master list. In contrast, former Federal Reserve Board Chair Paul Volcker had a key provision in the bill named after him and Harvard Law Professor Elizabeth Warren came up with the proposal for the new consumer financial protection agency. Both, without holding elected office, apparently had more influence in shaping the legislation than minority party members of the House of Representatives. As discussed later in this chapter, Republicans had more influence negotiating behind the scenes in the Senate, but most eventually chose to vote against the legislation for political reasons.

According to Kaiser, Frank was the most important figure in initiating the legislation; Senator Christopher Dodd (D-CT) is given credit mostly for shepherding it through the Senate. Kaiser, because he wrote from a congressional perspective, somewhat understates the role of the Obama administration. However, he acknowledges that Frank, during a meeting in February 2009, deferred to the new Obama administration in preparing an initial draft of the legislation (Kaiser 2013, 37 and 75).

The working group within the White House included well-known academics such as law professor and author Cass Sunstein, other legal professors, and financial institution experts in major positions in the Obama administration and at the Federal Reserve. Frank and his key committee staff director apparently were the only ones in Congress who were actively consulted, according to Kaiser. The working group also regularly met with high-ranking administrative officials such as Treasury Secretary Timothy Geithner, economic advisor Lawrence Summers, and Chief of Staff Rahm Emmanuel, who had been part of the Democratic leadership in the House before joining the Obama administration.

A concise, preliminary framework issued by the Department of Treasury in March 2009 outlined proposals to minimize systemic risks and emphasized the need for enhanced authority for the Treasury Department and the Federal Deposit Insurance Corporation (FDIC). University of Pennsylvania law professor David Skeel (2001, 49) criticized the provisions as reading "as if they had been written by Timothy Geithner in consultation with the large banks he had worked with as head of the New York Fed." A more detailed white paper written by the working group was released by the Department of Treasury on June 17 as *Financial Regulatory Reform - A New Foundation: Rebuilding Financial Supervision and Regulation*. While its eighty-eight pages did not include full legislative language, it did contain details on the major financial reforms supported by the Obama administration.

President Obama himself gave a twenty-minute prepared speech when he introduced the white paper to the media and the public in the East Room of the White House. Obama acknowledged potential opposition. He carefully argued that the proposal was a balanced approach that would promote financial stability, not upheaval, while providing protections against a new crisis. Obama claimed that the proposal represented the results of a collaborative process and included Senator Richard Shelby (R-AL) and Representative Spencer Bachus (R-AL), the ranking Republicans on the related congressional committees, as being among those involved:

> These proposals reflect intensive consultation with leaders in Congress, including those who are here today: Chairman Dodd and Chairman Frank, who, along with Senator Shelby and Representative Bachus, will be meeting with me throughout this process. They met with me earlier this year to jumpstart the discussion of reform. These reforms are also drawing on conversations with regulators, including those I met with this morning, as well as consumer advocates and business leaders, academic experts, and the broader public. (Obama 2009)

A mild surprise, addressed toward the end of Obama's speech, was support for the establishment of a consumer financial protection agency. The proposal omitted a version of a proposal promoted by Paul Volcker to reinstitute a ban on proprietary trading by banks (the Volcker Rule); Volcker had led a working group at the influential nonprofit Group of Thirty that had issued its own recommendations for reform (Group of Thirty 2009). The white paper also did not deal with reform of Fannie Mae and Freddie Mac, the government-supported enterprises (GSEs) that shared some of the blame for mortgage financing problems and were a special target of libertarian and conservative groups (e.g., Wallison 2013). The white paper matched up with the actual legislative proposal that was forwarded to Congress at the end of June.

How did the Obama administration manage to complete a white paper and legislative proposal five months after assuming office? The simple answer is that it had to draw upon the expertise of those who were already intimately familiar with, and a part of, the current system. The *New York Times* found that the attorneys from the financial services law firm of Davis Polk & Waldwell did a lot of the work in crafting legislative language that was then edited by staff with the working group (Becker and Morgenson 2009; Skeel 2011, 50).

It is relatively common for lobbyists or those connected with interest groups to be involved in promoting legislation or to even draft model legislation. This practice violates citizen expectations about open access and deliberative democracy, even though it is almost a necessity in this era of complicated legislation. Senator Dodd, in particular, expected the bill to be substantially revised, but it is estimated that about 90 percent of the original proposal made it through to enactment in spite of substantial rewriting (Anand 2011; Kaiser 2013).

Frank had officially introduced the bill less than two weeks after receiving the draft language. After spending several months promoting reelection campaigns for Financial Services Committee members, having committee briefings, and deciding to champion the consumer financial protection agency, Frank apparently incorrectly thought that his committee members were ready to quickly approve the legislation (Kaiser 2013, 115). He certainly anticipated opposition from the financial industry, the U.S. Chamber of Commerce, and the House Republicans, but some lobbyists from organizations like the American Banking Association cleverly decided to focus on opposition to the consumer agency and some House Democrats also had unanticipated reservations.

The legislation bogged down over the August recess and about twenty staff members spent countless hours working on refining and revising the bill; some obvious flaws with the consumer agency were taken out, but a lot of the work dealt with technical details and minutia about regulatory processes (Kaiser 2013, 154). Kaiser also uncovered details about how Frank cut a deal in late September with the president of the Independent Community Bankers Association that considerably reduced opposition to the bill and led to a November amendment by Representative Luis Gutierrez (D-IL) that more or less punished larger banks by increasing what they had to pay to the Federal Deposit Insurance Corporation while helping smaller banks (Kaiser 2013, 160–64). In general, supporting smaller banks and credit unions was a smart political strategy; it allowed Democratic legislators to simultaneously vilify Wall Street, claim support for smaller businesses, and to continue to receive donations from parts of the huge financial industry sector.

A revised draft was finally ready by early October and markup began in earnest in mid-October 2009. Both Democrats and Republicans offered amendments, but the only Republican amendment to pass was one that kept auto dealers from being subject to the new consumer agency. In hindsight, that defeat was probably a blessing in disguise since it kept the influential National Automobile Dealers Association mostly on the sidelines afterwards (Kaiser 2013, 176–79). Each section (title) of the proposed legislation was considered as a separate bill at this stage, with votes first on amendments and then the overall section. With lots of debate and discussion, it took a full month to get through markup. There was another delay on the last vote in early December as Frank unsuccessfully attempted to avoid a boycott by members of the Congressional Black Congress (CBC) (Kaiser 2013, 179–83). The entire legislation then had to be consolidated, with Frank adding and modifying provisions in response to concerns from the CBC about offering more relief to homeowners and minority-owned businesses. More moderate Democrats also wanted to see less federal preemption of state laws (Kaiser 2013, 183–88).

The entire legislative proposal went to the House Rules Committee led by Representative Louise Slaughter (D-NY). Kaiser (2013, 206) reported that House Speaker Nancy Pelosi's staff was responsible for suggesting the addition of "Wall Street Reform" to the title with Frank's approval. Therefore, the entire title was now the "The Wall Street Reform and Consumer Protection Act of 2009." The Rules Committee pared down 238 amendments to thirty-six and ended up approving about thirteen hours of debate, including three hours of general debate, two hours for committee members, an hour for other related committees, and six hours for amendments.

House floor debate began on the evening of December 9 as the Rules Committee was still meeting. At the request of Republicans, there was a recorded vote on the rules that began after 8 p.m., with voting predictably along party lines that passed 235–177. The three hours of general debate was more political theater than substance. As Frank wrapped up the speeches after midnight, Kaiser observed that: "there were three other Democrats and four Republicans on the floor, plus about a dozen staff. Just one person sat in the gallery, the author of this book [Kaiser], and a couple of dozen spectators were sprinkled around the public galleries" (Kaiser 2013, 220).

Consideration of the bill continued the following afternoon and, because of the late start, continued well into the evening. Probably by design, that schedule left the most significant votes for Friday, December 11. While Friday sessions are unusual as members prefer to travel back to their districts, the timing meant that the House was still done before the weekend and holiday season. A Republican amendment to delete the new consumer agency failed 208–223 and the overall bill passed by a similar margin, 223–202. Given the strong Democratic majority at the time, a number of moderate Democrats could afford to vote no and still have the bill pass (McCarty, Poole, and Rosenthal 2013, 209).

On the Senate side, Senator Dodd, chair of the Banking, Housing, and Urban Affairs Committee, attempted over the summer and fall of 2009 to get bipartisan support by working with Republican committee staff and Senator Shelby, the ranking minority member. Dodd apparently thought that committee review would be as smooth as what happened with the credit card legislation. He anticipated a quick review beginning in mid-November and committee approval by the end of the year, to catch up with the House of Representatives. Kaiser revealed that Dodd sent personal notes and called the Republican members of the committee ahead of a kick-off hearing a week before Thanksgiving (Kaiser 2013, 195). However, Senator Shelby criticized the process and Dodd was left with having to appoint bipartisan working groups rather than have Shelby as a true working partner.

Progress then stalled over the holidays and through the Senate votes on healthcare reform. Dodd apparently did a lot of soul-searching during this time and made an announcement in early January 2010 that he would not run for reelection (Kaiser 2013, 227–34). He made financial reform his top priority and his decision probably made it easier to get a bill through the Senate.

Even so, as Kaiser recounts it, there was a pattern of interaction with Shelby's staff that was confusing and frustrating. One staff member would signal willingness to compromise and offer proposals, while a second key staff person would refuse to negotiate and take a rigidly partisan position. Shelby himself often would make conflicting public and private comments, perhaps because of pressure from Republican Senate leaders to block Obama administration proposals.

There also was uncertainty about the degree to which Republican senators could block or significantly alter a financial reform bill. Democrats had a majority in the Senate, but lost their filibuster-proof supermajority after Republican Scott Brown won a special election in January 2010 to fill Senator Ted Kennedy's seat after his death from a brain tumor. According to political scientists Nolan McCarty, Keith Poole, and Howard Rosenthal (2013, 195), Brown was in the "pivot" or critical position on the proposed legislation.

The day after Obama's one-year anniversary as president, Obama made an eight-minute speech on financial reform to publicly endorse adding the Volcker Rule to financial legislation and oppose further mergers of large financial companies. He made a point to include Brown along with Frank and Dodd (Kaiser 2013, 238–39). The speech was also an exhortation to Congress to take action:

> My message to members of Congress of both parties is that we have to get this done. And my message to leaders of the financial industry is to work with us, and not against us, on needed reforms. I welcome constructive input from folks in the financial sector. But what we've seen so far, in recent weeks, is an army of industry lobbyists from Wall Street descending on Capitol Hill to try and block basic and commonsense rules of the road that would protect our economy and the American people.
>
> So if these folks want a fight, it's a fight I'm ready to have. And my resolve is only strengthened when I see a return to old practices at some of the very firms fighting reform; and when I see soaring profits and obscene bonuses at some of the very firms claiming that they can't lend more to small business, they can't keep credit card rates low, they can't pay a fee to refund taxpayers for the bailout without passing on the cost to shareholders or customers—that's the claims they're making. It's exactly this kind of irresponsibility that makes clear reform is necessary. (Obama 2010a)

Dodd did his part by further attempting to work with Republican senators, especially Bob Corker (R-TN). This process led to the development of an automatic funding provision for the consumer financial agency out of federal reserve funds (Kaiser 2013, 242–60); it was fiscally conservative, but ironically later impeded Republicans in their efforts to curtail or abolish the agency. Another irony is that Corker's proposal was incorporated into Dodd's bill without Corker's approval when Dodd decided to avoid further delays and move the legislation out of committee on March 22 without markup sessions, an almost unheard off action.

Dodd decided that it would be better to attempt bipartisan negotiations with a wider pool of senators to get to sixty votes, but this was easier said than done. Senate Minority Leader Mitch McConnell (R-KY) and Dodd exchanged angry speeches on financial reform in the Senate in April (Kaiser 2013, 268–72). Kaiser (2013, 299–303) also reported a flurry of communication between Dodd, Democratic leaders, Shelby's staff, and the pro-reform group Americans for Financial Reform that at various times threatened to halt the process. However, news coverage of an indictment against investment firm Goldman Sachs and a related Senate hearing made it increasingly difficult for Republicans to continue to block consideration of the legislation. Shelby and his staff were also able to get a major concession related to funding of costs to deal with banks seized and sold by the FDIC.

Dodd and his staff also had to deal with senators who could thwart passage if their recommendations were not included in the bill. For example, Blanche Lincoln (D-AK), chair of the Agriculture Committee, asked for additional derivative trading restrictions, with support from a few moderate senators such as Maria Cantwell (D-WA) and Olympia Snowe (R-ME). Kaiser (2013, 296–97) quotes a Banking Committee staff member as describing many of the inserted provisions as being mistakes that were not fully corrected in the final legislation.

The full Senate began considering the bill in early May and approved a variety of amendments, from both Democrats and Republicans. The Senate leadership attempted to close off debate on May 19 while several key amendments, such as a stronger Volcker Rule and an exemption to auto dealers, were still pending. The cloture vote failed with Senators Cantwell and Russ Feingold (D-WI) voting no and creating a need for more moderate Republican support. After intensively lobbying Senator Brown, debate could be closed off the next afternoon with the minimum 60 votes (Kaiser 2013, 318–19). The bill was finally voted upon in the evening. With two absences, two nays from Democrats (Cantwell and Feingold), and four yeas from moderate Republicans, the legislation advanced to a conference committee by a 59–39 vote. It bears repeating that the Republican senators most involved in negotiations over the bill, Shelby and Corker, voted against the legislation.

A conference committee process followed. Once commonplace and considered an essential part of the legislative process, it has been rarely used in the last few decades as the political parties have become more polarized and consensus decision-making has become next to impossible. On this bill, Representative Frank thought that a conference committee would not get bogged down with infighting among majority and minority members. He decided months in advance that a conference committee, chaired by him, would be the best way to finalize the legislation (Kaiser 2013, 332). In practical terms, the staff did most of the work in reconciling and refining the very detailed and complicated House and Senate bills. Paul Volcker, Senator Brown, Senator Lincoln, the Congressional Black Caucus, and the Treasury staff were among those who had influence in shaping the final version.

Conference committee discussion and a series of votes took place over two weeks in June, with the proceedings televised on C-SPAN. The final conference committee votes, including adding Dodd-Frank to the name of the legislation, passed around 5:40 a.m. on June 25 after a marathon session to avoid any final roadblocks. Kaiser (2013, 357) commented that there were a few other reporters in attendance, but that "no one in the room could remember such an important congressional event occurring at such a preposterous hour." Even with the scheduling designed to deter opposition, Senator Brown then demanded that a $19 billion bank fee be removed; his support was so crucial to Senate passage that the conference committee was briefly reopened to deal with his concern (Kaiser 2013, 359–61).

The renamed Dodd-Frank Wall Street Reform and Consumer Protection Act of 2010 (Dodd-Frank Act) was at last ready for final consideration by both chambers of Congress a year after its introduction. Working around memorials for Senator Robert Byrd (D-WV) and the Independence Day holiday, the House had its final vote on June 30 and picked up a few more Republican votes, resulting in passage by a vote of 237-192. Based on ideology, three Republicans voting in favor was unexpected, but they were more moderate than many of their colleagues (McCarty, Poole, and Rosenthal 2013, 211). The Senate approved Dodd-Frank on July 15 by a 60–39 vote, almost identical to its vote in May. Cantwell voted for the bill this time, but Feingold continued to be a maverick. Based just on ideology, a few more Republican senators might have voted for the bill, but there was not a need for them to go against their leadership (McCarty, Poole, and Rosenthal 2013, 212–14).

President Obama signed the Dodd-Frank Act on July 21, 2010, in an elaborate ceremony that was held in an auditorium in the Ronald Reagan building, not the usual White House location. A few months ahead of midterm elections that would shrink the Democratic majority in the Senate and result in a Republican majority in the House, Obama's speech reflected his growing recognition of the fading prospects for bipartisanship during his tenure as president:

> For the last year, Chairmen Barney Frank and Chris Dodd have worked day and night—(applause)—Barney and Chris have worked day and night to bring about this reform. And I am profoundly grateful to them. I would be remiss if I didn't also express my appreciation to Senator Harry Reid and Speaker Nancy Pelosi for their leadership. It wouldn't have happened without them. (Applause.)
>
> Passing this bill was no easy task. To get there, we had to overcome the furious lobbying of an array of powerful interest groups and a partisan minority determined to block change. So the members who are here today, both on the stage and in the audience, they have done a great service in devoting so much time and expertise to this effort, to looking out for the public interests and not the special interests. (Applause.) And I also want to thank the three Republican senators who put partisanship aside—(applause)—judged this bill on the merits, and voted for reform. We're grateful to them. (Applause.) And the Republican House members. (Obama 2010b)

STORY WITHIN A STORY: THE CONSUMER FINANCIAL PROTECTION BUREAU (CFPB)

Before moving on to reflection about the passage of Dodd-Frank and implementation issues, the establishment of the Consumer Financial Protection Bureau (CFPB) warrants a closer examination. While it was adopted as one of the titles within Dodd-Frank (Title X), it had a unique path from conceptualization to enactment. The proposal is a rarity in that it can be so clearly traced to a particular person and a moment in time. The concept of the agency first appeared as an article written by Elizabeth Warren, then a Harvard University law professor, in a start-up journal, *Democracy* (Warren 2007), just ahead of the worst of the financial crisis; a revised version was published in 2008 in the *Journal of Consumer Affairs* (Warren 2008).

Remarkably, the proposal survived relatively intact through the legislative process, became law within three years, and its originator was able to lead the implementation efforts. Warren's deceptively simple proposal was one of those ideas that burst upon the public's consciousness with such drama and intensity that they create an inevitable demand for change. One day the issue is barely even discussed; if it is talked about at all it is within a small policy community. The next day it is motivating the entire society to action (Kamarck 2013, 31).

Elaine Kamarck, in her 2013 book on policy change, uses the example of how the publication of Rachel Carson's *Silent Spring* led to the banning of the pesticide DDT (Kamarck 2013, 31-34). The success of Warren's proposal followed a similar path. Both wrote in accessible styles and caught the attention of congressional leaders and sympathetic presidents. Carson's (1962) haunting vision of a community so polluted that a time would come when birds would no longer return in spring continues to resonate over fifty years later, partially because that possibility still exists. Warren used a memorable narrative as well.

Warren chose to compare financial instruments to toasters. In her 2014 autobiography, she called it a simple idea based on her experience as a young mother when she forgot about bread in a toaster and it caught fire (Warren 2014, 127). Similarly, you should be able to purchase a loan knowing that it is safe and will not "explode" and leave you without a home (Warren 2007). Warren further emphasized the analogy by titling her article "Unsafe at Any Rate," connecting it to Ralph Nader's classic 1965 book, *Unsafe at Any Speed,* about the need to regulate safety in the automobile industry. Just as the U.S. Consumer Product Safety Commission, established in 1972, now protects consumers from products that are unsafe, she argued that America needed a Financial Product Safety Commission to regulate financial products and services so consumers would not be harmed.

Warren was different from Carson, though, in being comfortable with advocacy and being willing to actively draw upon connections with elected leaders. Warren had served on the National Bankruptcy Review Commission from 1995 to 1997, which gave her the opportunity to learn about the political process and how to run federal commissions. In 1998, she cultivated the support of the lion of the Senate, Ted Kennedy (D-MA), who remained an ally until his death in 2009 (Warren 2014, 61–64). Warren also published several well-known books about bankruptcy and debt (including two with her daughter), branching out from more legal textbooks and academic research studies.

Warren was selected by Senate Majority Leader Harry Reid (D-NV) in late 2008 to be part of the congressional oversight panel for the financial bailout legislation and, thus, was in regular communication with congressional and administration leaders (Warren 2014, 83–126). It probably helped Warren's cause that legislators had overwhelmingly adopted updated consumer product legislation through the Consumer Product Safety Improvement Act of 2008 (H.R. 4040, PL 110-314) just a few months before the financial crisis hit.

Warren mentions meeting with AFL-CIO leaders and Senator Kennedy in February 2009. In April, she met Barney Frank at his apartment in Massachusetts and also discussed the proposal with economic advisor Larry Summers over dinner in Washington, D.C. In between, Senator Kennedy and a few other senators introduced a bill to signal support for the agency and President Obama used the toaster analogy in a talk show interview (Warren 2014, 106, 131–44).

Warren was part of the White House event in June 2009 to announce the administration's financial reform proposal. She then teamed with Dan Geldon of the Roosevelt Institute (and a former member of the oversight panel) to work with Americans for Financial Reform, other interest groups, and members of Congress (Warren 2014, 144–52). McCarty, Poole, and Rosenthal (2013, 187) reproduced the only official photo of President Obama with Warren to demonstrate his apparent ambivalence about consumer-oriented reform, but Warren herself (2014, 146) emphatically stated in her autobiography that she learned that Obama "believed passionately that the White House needed to support a reform measure that would help regular people, and he saw the agency as the best way to do it."

According to Kaiser, Frank became an enthusiastic supporter of Warren and saw her support as a good barometer of how more liberal interest groups and Congress members were reacting to the proposed financial reform legislation. Warren describes being summoned by Frank to a fall meeting with a small group of legislators and, in response to a question, was able to get credit-reporting agency oversight added to the proposal for the new agency (Warren 2014, 152–54). Warren didn't seem to have as much direct access to the Senate, but vocally supported Dodd's efforts to keep the agency in the legislation. The automatic funding provisions through Federal Reserve funds (about $500 million a year) and relative autonomy that were part of the Senate bill gave the new agency a strong foundation. At the signing ceremony in July 2010, Warren had a front-row seat and received one of the eleven pens used to sign the bill (Warren 2014, 160–61).

That level of inside access and influence was truly extraordinary and continued further into 2010. Warren met with President Obama in August and again in September 2010 as a prelude to being appointed a special advisor to help start up the Consumer Financial Protection Bureau (CFPB) (Warren 2014, 167–72). She really was the de facto founding director, but her popularity among liberals made her equally unpopular among conservatives and unconfirmable by the Senate.

Richard (Rich) Cordray, a former attorney general of Ohio and first enforcement officer for the CFPB, was nominated as director in the summer of 2011, but was also opposed by Republicans; he was given a recess appointment and eventually confirmed by the full Senate in 2013 for a five-year term. Meanwhile, Warren ran for the U.S. Senate and defeated Senator Brown by a substantial margin in November 2012. When Senator John Kerry (D-MA) was appointed Secretary of State, Warren became the senior senator from Massachusetts and has cemented her standing as a national political figure.

KEY PROVISIONS OF DODD-FRANK AND IMPLEMENTATION ISSUES

There are a myriad of ways to categorize and evaluate the Dodd-Frank Act. Kaiser (2013, 379), as a Washington Beltway journalist, labeled it as "quite a good bill that will have sweeping consequences." Congressional Republicans and more libertarian interests argue that Dodd-Frank has unnecessarily expanded the scope of government and did not deal with root causes of the financial crisis (Wallison 2013). There is some truth to this assertion as Congress' own Financial Crisis Inquiry Commission (2011) did not finish its work until six months after the passage of Dodd-Frank and concluded with the four members appointed by Republicans dissenting from the final report.

Dodd-Frank's extreme length and complexity are another source of criticism. One source claims that the Act is a slightly more digestible 848 pages rather than the over two thousand pages commonly cited (Anand 2011, xv). Another legal reference book manages to reproduce the act in seven hundred pages using a small but still readable font (CCH 2010).

According to law professor David Skeel, two major approaches shape Dodd-Frank: a reliance on the financial industry as a partner and continued ad hoc approaches to crises. Skeel (2011, 8) argues that "each could dangerously distort American finance, making it more politically charged, less vibrant, and further removed from basic rule-of-law principles than ever before in modern American financial history." The Act also contains a number of miscellaneous provisions, which is unfortunately typical of omnibus legislation. Berson and Derson (2012, 1–2) cite requirements for companies to disclose energy extraction payments made to other countries and to track materials mined from countries with human rights problems. These items and a requirement for new Minority and Women Inclusion offices were part of a package of items promoted by the CBC and especially Representative Maxine Waters (D-CA), a member of the House Financial Services Committee (McCarty, Poole, and Rosenthal 2013, 198).

Even if there had not been congressional and interest group attempts to modify its provisions, Dodd-Frank builds in complicated and lengthy implementation that make it a "living legislation" (Jenkins and Patashnik 2012). According to Anand (2011, 93), "The bill has more than 240 rulemaking provisions, sixty-seven one-time reports of studies, and directs the preparation of an additional twenty-two periodic reports." His handbook, *The Essentials of the Dodd-Frank Act*, distills the major rulemaking deadlines and effective dates into an even dozen (Anand 2011). A more complete listing runs twenty-five pages and lists almost three hundred separate effective dates (CCH 2010).

Davis Polk & Waldwell, the same legal firm that had a hand in drafting the legislation, has tracked the rulemaking process through a series of reports posted on its website, www.davispolk.com, and a more detailed subscription service. Only 37 percent of deadlines had been met as of the 2013 third-anniversary report, but the compliance rate was up to 55 percent by 2014 and included regulations on the Volcker Rule. According to Davis Polk's calculations, rulemaking was about 75 percent complete (208 of 398).

Eric Patashnik and Julian Zelizer (2013, 1082) have used the old adage "death by a thousand cuts" to describe the rulemaking process. There has been intense lobbying over the rules and the existing regulatory structure, with a multitude of agencies, remains fragmented and has been relatively underfunded due to Republican opposition. Skeel (2011, 155) says, "There is no politically plausible scenario under which its key planks will be reversed, however much its opponents hope that shifts in Congress will make this an option in the coming years." Patashnik and Zelizer pretty much agree that the large financial companies have mastered the details of Dodd-Frank and may not desire major change. Still, it is difficult to predict partisan tides and the outcome of legal challenges to major legislation (Berry, Burden, and Howell 2010; Maltzman and Shipan 2008).

Counter-intuitively, Patashnik and Zelizer are fairly optimistic about the future of the Consumer Financial Protection Bureau, which has been much more obviously under political attack. Republican opponents have regularly introduced bills that would repeal or weaken the CFPB (Consumer Federation of America 2014; Dennis 2011). Early proposals would have greatly altered the scope and authority of the CFPB by replacing the director with a five-member commission and removing the automatic funding provisions in favor of congressional appropriation (Wilmarth 2012). Recent proposals do not appear to be as extensive, consistent with historical analyses of legislation that have found that the probability of repeal peaks shortly after adoption and then declines over time (Berry, Burden, and Howell 2010; Ragusa 2010).

The CFPB may be entrenched by the end of Obama administration and "it has the chance to build an organizational reputation as a trusted consumer advocate, and gain power over time" (Patashnik and Zelizer 2013, 1082). From a cursory review of its website, the CFPB appears to be a well-established, twenty-first-century agency. It has an easy process for submitting complaints and telling financial stories, social media links, resources for paying for college, and announcements about workshops around the country. It has a fully developed organizational chart with 45 different boxes and a clear, mission-driven strategic plan. The CFPB is even making its complaint database available to academics for analysis (Ayres, Lingwall, and Steinway 2014).

CONCLUSION

Many of the key actors in the passage of Dodd-Frank have exited the political stage and this legislation was their swan song. As alluded to earlier, Sen. Dodd retired at the end of 2010 and since then has been the chair and chief executive officer of the Motion Picture Association of America, which includes promoting film interests to Congress. Rep. Frank retired in 2012, but continues to regularly make appearances on political television shows. Sen. Lincoln lost her reelection bid in 2010 and, as previously mentioned, Sen. Brown lost to Elizabeth Warren in 2012. For Warren, Dodd-Frank and the creation of the CFPB made her a household name in her early sixties and a place in the annals of consumer advocacy.

While it is tempting to conclude that Congress still works and to acknowledge the herculean efforts of Dodd-Frank supporters, one is left with a sense of a flawed democracy and a lack of confidence about whether many of its provisions will be effective in safeguarding the financial system. Going back to more old-style, simpler laws that could be easily updated seems preferable to murky, dense legislation that takes years to implement and even longer to evaluate. McCarty, Poole, and Rosenthal (2013, 20) make an appealing argument for "a strong set of simple rules with regulatory discretion. The thirty-seven pages of Glass-

Steagall [now repealed Depression Era financial reform] are much to be preferred to the nearly three thousand pages of Dodd-Frank." Only the creation of the CFPB seems to meet that criterion of simplicity, with its guaranteed funding and clearly stated mission to "make markets for consumer financial products and services work for Americans—whether they are applying for a mortgage, choosing among credit cards, or using any number of other consumer financial products."

The rest of Dodd-Frank's provisions remain unknown to most Americans and even the CFPB faces an uncertain future. With financial reform we are just past the third step of a messy process toward fulfillment of what political scientist James Morone (1990) has called the "democratic wish." We moved from stalemate to popular response and then to the creation of a new institution. We are not able to predict the parameters of the fourth and last step, a settling of political and governmental institutions that may or may not really be a move toward a "stronger, more competent public sphere" (Morone 1990, 332).

NOTES

Kristen Endow provided graduate research assistance for this chapter.

1. Bill histories are available at thomas.loc.gov. The Credit Card Act was considered by the 111th Congress as H.R. 627. The final version was enrolled as Public Law 111-024. Information on the law's major provisions and implementation are available on the Consumer Financial Protection Bureau's website.

REFERENCES

Adler, E. Scott, and John D. Wilkerson. 2012. *Congress and the Politics of Problem Solving*. New York: Cambridge University Press.

Anand, Sanjay. 2011. *Essentials of the Dodd-Frank Act*. Hoboken, NJ: John Wiley.

Ayres, Ian, Jeff Lingwall, and Sonia Steinway. 2014. "Skeletons in the Database: An Early Analysis of the CFPB's Consumer Complaints." *Fordham Journal of Corporate & Financial Law* 19: 343–90.

Becker, Jo, and Gretchen Morgenson. 2009. "Member and Overseer of Finance Club." *New York Times*, April 27.

Berry, Christopher R., Barry C. Burden, and William G. Howell. 2010. "After Enactment: The Lives and Deaths of Federal Programs." *American Journal of Political Science* 54: 1–17.

Berson, Susan, and Dave Derson. 2012. *The Dodd-Frank Wall Street Reform and Consumer Protection Act: From Legislation to Implementation to Litigation*. Chicago: American Bar Association Publishing.

Carson, Rachel. 1962. *Silent Spring*. Boston, MA: Houghton Mifflin.

CCH Attorney-Editor Staff. 2010. *Dodd-Frank Wall Street Reform and Consumer Protection Act: Law, Explanation, and Analysis*. Chicago: Wolters Kluwer Law and Business.

Consumer Federation of America. 2014. *House Hearing Considers Eleven Bills that Would Weaken the Consumer Financial Protection Bureau and Consumer Protections*, May 21.

Dennis, Brady. 2011. "One Year Later, Frank Pleased with Overhaul." *Washington Post*, July 12.

Financial Crisis Inquiry Commission. 2011. *Financial Crisis Commission Report*. Washington, D.C.: Government Printing Office.

Group of Thirty, Working Group on Financial Reform. 2009. *Financial Reform: A Framework for Financial Stability*. Washington, D.C.: Group of Thirty.

Jenkins, Jeffrey A., and Eric M. Patashnik, eds. 2012. *Living Legislation: Durability, Change, and the Politics of American Lawmaking*. Chicago: University of Chicago Press.

Kaiser, Robert G. 2013. *Act of Congress: How America's Essential Institution Works, and How It Doesn't*. New York: Knopf.

Kamarck, Elaine C. 2013. *How Change Happens – or Doesn't: The Politics of US Public Policy*. Boulder, CO: Lynne Rienner.

Library of Congress. N.D. [database of congressional legislation] thomas.loc.gov.

Maltzman, Forrest, and Charles R. Shipan. 2008. "Change, Continuity, and the Evolution of the Law." *American Journal of Political Science* 52: 252–67.

Mayhew, David R. 2006. "Congress as Problem Solver." In *Promoting the General Welfare: New Perspectives on Government Performance*, edited by Alan S. Gerber and Eric M. Patashnik, 219-36. Washington, D.C.: Brookings Institution.

McCarty, Nolan, Keith T. Poole, and Howard Rosenthal. 2013. *Political Bubbles: Financial Crises and the Failure of American Democracy*. Princeton, NJ: Princeton University Press.

Morone, James A. 1990. *The Democratic Wish: Popular Participation and the Limits of American Government*. New York: Basic.

Obama, Barack. 2009. *Remarks by the President on 21st Century Financial Regulatory Reform*. Washington, D.C.: The White House Office of the Press Secretary, June 17.

Obama, Barack. 2010a. *Remarks by the President on Financial Reform*. Washington, D.C.: The White House Office of the Press Secretary, January 21.

Obama, Barack. 2010b. *Remarks by the President at Signing of Dodd-Frank Wall Street Reform and Consumer Protection Act*. Washington, D.C.: The White House Office of the Press Secretary, July 21.

Patashnik, Eric M. 2008. *Reforms at Risk: What Happens after Major Policies Are Enacted*. Princeton: Princeton University Press.

Patashnik, Eric M., and Julian E. Zelizer. 2013. "The Struggle to Remake Politics: Liberal Reform and the Limits of Policy Feedback in the Contemporary American State." *Perspectives on Politics* 11: 1071–87.

Polk, Davis. 2014. *Dodd-Frank Progress Report*. New York: Davis Polk & Wardwell LLP, July 18.

Ragusa, Jordan. 2010. "The Lifecycle of Public Policy: An Event History Analysis of Repeals to Landmark Legislative Enactments, 1951–2006." *American Politics Research* 38:1015-51.

Sinclair, Barbara. 2012. *Unorthodox Lawmaking: New Legislative Processes in the U.S. Congress*. 4th ed. Washington, D.C.: Congressional Quarterly.

Skeel, David. 2011. *The New Financial Deal: Understanding the Dodd-Frank Act and Its (Unintended) Consequences*. Hoboken, NJ: John Wiley.

U.S. Department of the Treasury. 2009a. *Financial Regulatory Reform, New Foundation: Rebuilding Financial Supervision and Regulation*.

U.S. Department of the Treasury. 2009b. *Treasury Outlines Framework for Regulatory Reform*, press release.

Wallison, Peter J. 2013. *Bad History, Worse Policy: How a False Narrative about the Financial Crisis Led to the Dodd-Frank Act*. Washington, D.C.: American Enterprise Institute.

Warren, Elizabeth. 2007. "Unsafe at Any Rate." *Democracy* 1: 8–19.

Warren, Elizabeth. 2008. "Product Safety Regulation as a Model for Financial Services Regulation." *Journal of Consumer Affairs* 42: 452–60.

Warren, Elizabeth. 2014. *A Fighting Chance*. New York: Henry Holt.

Wilmarth, Arthur E. 2012. "The Financial Services Industry's Misguided Quest to Undermine the Consumer Financial Protection Bureau." *Review of Banking and Financial Law* 31: 881–956.

EIGHT

The USA PATRIOT Act (2001)

Kevin N. Buterbaugh

On the morning of September 11, 2001, nineteen hijackers took over four planes leaving from Boston, Newark, and Dulles airports. The hijackers planned to use the planes as weapons flying them into major buildings in the United States. Two thousand, nine hundred and seventy-seven people lost their lives in the attacks, while almost 9,000 people were injured (Johnston 2013). The attacks also caused more than $20 billion worth of damage to property, and tens of billions of dollars of damage to the U.S. economy (Templeton and Lumley 2002). These attacks were the largest and most damaging terrorist attacks in history, as well as the most damaging by a foreign power on U.S. soil, eclipsing the attack on Pearl Harbor by the Japanese on December 7, 1941.

Six weeks after the attack, the U.S. Congress responded by passing the USA PATRIOT Act on votes of 98–1 in the Senate and 357–66 in the House (Howell 2004, 1145–1207). One should not be surprised that Congress acted after the attack. What is surprising is the speed of Congress' action. For example, it took Congress almost a year after the Oklahoma City bombing of 1995 to pass a bill, and for much of that bill, Congress had been working on since the first World Trade Center bombing in 1993.

The speed of congressional action should also make one wonder how Congress knew what to reform or change since the 9/11 Commission was not established until a year after the attacks, and it did not report its findings until 2004. No other studies were completed to evaluate the attacks prior to passage of the legislation.

How did a law as lengthy (more than 130 pages), complex, and important as the USA PATRIOT Act pass in such a short amount of time? What does its passage tell us about the federal policymaking process? How has the law been implemented? What controversies have resulted from its implementation? What have the courts said about the law and its implementation by the executive branch? These are the questions the rest of this chapter will answer.

GARBAGE CANS AND POLICYMAKING

John Kingdon (1990), in his book *Agendas, Alternatives, and Public Policies*, argues that laws are often the result of irrational processes. This means that policymakers do not sit down and list their goals, assess the options for achieving those goals, and then choose the option that provides the best outcome. Instead, what drives policy is the confluence of three streams: a problem stream, a solution stream, and a politics stream. These streams come together in a "garbage can," a place or forum where a decision can be made. Thus, a garbage can is a committee in Congress, a federal commission that makes rules, or any other place that has the authority to actually come to a decision. The metaphor of a garbage can is used to highlight the fact that what comes out of the process may be a surprise. When the three streams mix, like garbage in a can, almost anything may result.

The problem stream consists of issues that various political actors will want to change or ameliorate. The fact that a situation exists that is negative or harmful does not mean it will be considered a problem. For example, each year thousands of Americans are killed in automobile crashes. However, the number of deaths per year has been falling steadily over the last few decades. Thus, instead of thousands of deaths being seen as a problem, policymakers may view the issue as showing that current policies are working and no reforms or changes are needed. This means that those who wish to accelerate the decline in deaths will have trouble convincing other policymakers that there is a problem.

Moreover, decision-makers have only so much time and energy to spare. The result is that issues that all believe are a problem may not get a solution, since something more important to the decision-makers is addressed instead. In cases such as these, a policymaker who wants something done must provide some evidence that the problem is important enough to warrant change, or the policymaker must find a way to re-frame the problem so that policymakers will want to address it. For example, if deaths in automobile accidents are seen as a problem of driver error, there will be little that government can do to reduce them. However, if the deaths are seen as caused by deficient cars or unsafe highways, then government policy may help. Thus, a person wanting change will need to re-frame the issue from one of driver error to one of car or highway safety if action is to occur. This can be done through argument and the provision of evidence.

More importantly, an issue can be re-framed or pushed up the ladder of importance through a focusing event. A focusing event is a crisis or a disaster that a political actor can use to re-frame or push an issue into public view. September 11 was a focusing event. Various policymakers could use it to re-frame and change the views of people on the problems confronting the country. While many could attempt to use it, only some succeed. One will see how it was used to re-frame issues in the section describing the making of the USA PATRIOT Act below.

The solution stream consists of various policies and ideas. Kingdon argues that these solutions are often looking for a problem to solve. Thus, one solution may be to deregulate and loosen the rules on private business in order to enhance economic growth. This solution may be latched onto any problem. Thus, it is possible that someone in attempting to reduce auto accidents argues that in fact the problem is one of too much regulation of automakers and that fewer rules will lead to more innovation, less red tape, and ultimately lower death rates. Various people will have pet solutions. What they will seek to do is to connect these pet solutions to any problem, whether it will fix the problem or not.

Kingdon argues that focusing events create "policy windows" for someone with a pet solution to connect to a new or re-framed problem that resulted from the event. In essence, Kingdon is telling us that when a crisis occurs, we should not expect a solution to be created specifically to solve it. Instead, someone will draw out of the solution stream a policy that already exists and connect it to the crisis. A solution must have some chance of reducing or ameliorating the problem to be chosen, but it can be far from the optimal solution. This means that there may be other solutions that would be a better fit for the problem, but if a group or person is not there to advocate for them, or to link them to the problem, then they will not be tried.

Finally, one comes to the politics stream. This consists of things like the national mood, the players involved in policymaking, and the energy of the players. It is possible that a crisis occurs that redefines a problem, a solution is available that can be connected to the problem, but the national mood will not support policy change, or that the people involved in the decision-making process do not have the energy or desire to make the change. National moods are difficult to determine, but Kingdon states that policymakers are aware of them and believe they are important. Mood is determined by attitudes amongst elites, groups attentive to policymaking, and occasionally the general public.

From this view of policymaking, the mix of problems, solutions, and participants in a garbage can determines what policy gets made, not by a rational selection process. Thus, policy can be a surprise, much as what comes out of a real garbage can be a surprise once things are mixed up in it.

THE MAKING OF THE USA PATRIOT ACT

On the morning of September 12, 2001, Assistant Attorney General Viet Dinh chaired a meeting of Justice Department personnel to task them with creating a package of new rules that would strengthen the hand of national law enforcement. Dinh stated to his colleagues, "Beginning immediately we will work a package of new authorities . . . the charge from Ashcroft [Attorney General] was very clear: 'all that is necessary for law enforcement, within the bounds of the Constitution, to discharge the obligation to fight this war against terror'" (O'Harrow 2002). Dinh then inquired of those at the meeting what problems they faced in fighting terrorism and possible solutions for these problems. Over the next several days, Dinh received a laundry list of solutions. Many of these had been in existence for years, and many had also been turned down as policy in the past (O'Harrow 2002). It should also be noted that while the United States had determined that Al Qaeda was behind the attacks by the evening of 9/11, it did not know how the attacks had been planned, who the actual hijackers were, or how they had managed to pull off the attack when the initial list of reforms was created.

Congress also moved rapidly into action after the attack. Again, on September 12, Congress passed a joint resolution condemning the attacks, and on September 14, it authorized the president the use of force against those behind the attack. Congress also passed a series of amendments to an appropriations act—labeled the Combating Terrorism Act—on September 13 which directed the Justice Department to conduct four studies related to terrorism and it expanded the government's ability to wire tap and electronically surveil suspected terrorists (Howell 2004, 1145–1207).

At the same time, Senator Patrick Leahy (D-VT), chairman of the Senate Judiciary Committee, began work on his own terrorism legislation. He had received word that the Justice Department was preparing a package of rules changes, and he wanted to have something in response. Leahy feared that the Justice Department's proposal would expand federal powers too dramatically and would have too broad an impact on civil liberties in the United States. By creating his own bill, he hoped to temper what the executive branch proposed (Howell 2004, 1145–1207).

On Monday, September 17, Attorney General Ashcroft asked Congress to pass his proposed legislation within the week, even though the proposal was still in the process of being drafted. He stated that he expected it to be completed on Wednesday, September 19, for congressional action (Shenon 2001, B4). Ashcroft warned that a threat may continue to exist in the United States, and that new powers were needed to uncover and fight them (Howell 2004, 1145–1207). Congressional leaders made clear to Ashcroft that while they would move swiftly on any proposed legislation, they would not pass anything that week.

The White House also slowed Ashcroft down. Ashcroft had failed to provide the White House a copy of his proposal. When a copy was finally provided, the staff was surprised by the proposal's scope. It went well beyond Justice Department jurisdiction, yet none of the other affected agencies had been consulted or given their approval. Ashcroft was forced to clean the proposal and to apologize to the White House for exceeding his authority (Brill 2003).

A coalition of groups worried about civil liberties also began to form hoping to slow down the legislation and weaken its provisions. The coalition was quite aware that its task would be difficult. The American people were afraid, and security was seen as more important than civil liberties. A statement signed by 150 groups called on Congress and the policymakers to have "'faith in our democratic system and our Constitution, and in our ability to protect at the same time both freedom and security of all Americans'" (qtd. in O'Harrow 2002).[1] In the end, the coalition was largely unsuccessful.

As promised, Ashcroft formally presented his proposal on September 19 to the leadership of the judiciary committees of the House and Senate. His proposal, the Antiterrorism Act of 2001 (ATA), was forty pages long and contained five major sections.

The first section proposed changes to the Foreign Intelligence Surveillance Act (FISA) of 1978. FISA had created a secret court that oversaw intelligence activities in the United States. Specifically, it was used to obtain warrants in intelligence cases to wiretap, examine pen registers,[2] and perform sneak and peek searches.[3] Ashcroft's proposal called for the loosening of rules on these activities. By making these actions easier to perform, Ashcroft argued that terrorism could be prevented.

The second section proposed amending immigration laws to make it easier to detain, deport, and share information about aliens in the United States. Ashcroft wanted the ability to indefinitely detain immigrants if they were suspected of having a connection to terrorist groups or acts. The third section dealt with changes to criminal laws and procedures. This would create new terrorism-related crimes, expand the scope of old terrorism-related crimes, and change the punishment for terrorism and related crimes.

The fourth section dealt with changes to the money laundering laws of the United States. Here, the Justice Department proposed new definitions for aiding terrorist groups financially and asked for the expansion of authority for law enforcement agents to access tax and other financial records of individuals in order to track and control the movement of illicit sources of terrorism funds. Finally, the Justice Department asked for authority to pay rewards, to pay overtime to personnel involved in terror investigations, and to financially assist other countries cooperating in U.S. efforts against terror (Howell 2004, 1145–1207).

An earlier draft of the proposal had been sent to Congressman James Sensenbrenner (R-WI), chairman of the House Judiciary Committee. Sensenbrenner recalled examining the earlier draft on the evening of September 17. That draft not only called for the changes listed above, but also proposed the elimination of habeas corpus for the duration of the emergency. Habeas corpus is a fundamental right within the U.S. justice system. It allows people to challenge their detention and demand they be presented with evidence for their detention and charged with a crime or released. Eliminating habeas corpus for the duration of the emergency would mean that the government could hold American citizens without being charged and with no rights to challenge their detention. Sensenbrenner was shocked by the proposal and called Ashcroft to warn him that any proposal sent to Congress would be dead on arrival if it contained that provision. Since the proposal released on the 19th did not contain the provision, it seems clear that Ashcroft followed Sensenbrenner's advice (Brill 2003).

However, the ATA did see the curtailment of judicial review over much of the new authorities that would be granted to the executive branch. Ashcroft wanted the FBI and intelligence agencies to be able to collect on their own authority information that had required FISA court permission. For instance, prior to 9/11, the FBI could ask for business records like call logs from phone companies with FISA permission. Ashcroft's bill proposed allowing the FBI to collect this type of information with no FISA permission under certain circumstances. Also, it was proposed to allow grand jury testimony to be shared with intelligence agencies, and that the determination of what to share and with whom be completely outside of judicial review.

Sen. Leahy presented a draft of his legislation on September 19. His bill was labeled the Uniting and Strengthening America Act (USA Act). It contained several provisions or sections that Ashcroft's proposal did not. These were an increase of northern border control agents, a special counter-terrorism fund for the Department of Justice, an increase in the number of FISA Court judges, increased funding for the FBI, and an expansion of a law enforcement regional information sharing program. His proposal also created new crimes of terrorism. Finally, Leahy's bill offered different methods for handling money laundering and dealing with electronic surveillance and search and seizure with respect to terrorism and foreign intelligence operations. Leahy's bill was far more protective of individual rights and gave the courts a far larger role in review of executive actions.

Normally, legislation in Congress is first proposed by a member, and then sent to the relevant committee for hearings and markup. In the case of the USA PATRIOT Act, this procedure was sidestepped entirely in the Senate, and mostly in the House. Sen. Leahy and the Senate Judiciary Committee staff began negotiating directly with Ashcroft and the White

House after the unveiling of the proposals on September 19. The final product of these negotiations was eventually presented to the full Senate for a vote. However, formal legislation was never sent to Leahy's committee for hearings or to allow members an opportunity for markup.[4] Leahy's judiciary committee did hold one day of hearings on September 25 regarding Ashcroft's proposed bill. However, Ashcroft spent less than two hours with the committee, and most of his testimony dealt with the actions that the Justice Department had taken since 9/11, not the specifics of the legislation he had proposed. In the end, most senators did not get to ask Ashcroft questions about his proposal. And, Ashcroft was vague in response to questions he did receive. Moreover, Ashcroft used the hearing to argue that congressional delay on his bill was endangering the country (Howell 2004, 1145–1207).

After the Senate hearing on September 25, Sen. Leahy, and Senator Orrin Hatch (R-UT), the ranking Republican on the Senate Judiciary Committee, continued to negotiate with Ashcroft and various executive branch personnel over the next five days. These negotiations culminated in an agreement on September 30. However, at a meeting on September 30 to finalize the details of the agreement, Ashcroft changed his mind, and removed his support from parts of the agreement. Leahy responded by sending his staff back to the table to renegotiate. He was not willing to accept that the attorney general could roll back part of the agreement while allowing the parts he liked to stand. This led to further delay in the bill's passage in the Senate. Ashcroft and President Bush used this delay to attack the Senate and blame it for not passing legislation that would allow the federal government to properly counter the terrorist threat. Ashcroft stated to the press on October 2 that, "'I've asked Congress very clearly for additional tools to reduce the risk of further incidents. And I believe it is time for us to understand that tools can reduce the risk of terrorism, talk won't'" (qtd. in Howell 2004, 1165). Republican senators also publically blamed Sen. Leahy and the Democrats for delaying the legislation.

On October 2, the USA Act was officially introduced in the Senate. However, work continued on the bill over the next week, and work was so frantic that instead of having the complete bill printed and distributed amongst members, the Senate leadership had the Congressional Record print daily versions of the bill. It should be noted that several Senate committees and subcommittees held hearings dealing with various sections of Ashcroft's and Leahy's proposals and their consequences on civil rights and other issues. However, no committee was assigned the bill for formal markup. On October 9, then Senate Democratic Whip Harry Reid (Nevada) stated that the USA Act would be held at the desk. This means that the full Senate would examine the bill and then vote on it (Howell 2004, 1145–1207).

At the same time, Senator Tom Daschle (D-SD), then the majority leader of the Senate, sought unanimous consent to bring the bill to the floor for a vote on October 10. He asked that no amendments be allowed unless there was unanimous consent to those amendments. Thus, a single no on an amendment could block it. Sen. Daschle's proposed process for the floor vote led to discussion, negotiation, and delay. The bill would not make it to the floor of the Senate until October 11. It was agreed that four amendments would be allowed, to be proposed by Senator Russ Feingold (D-WI) as well as one manager's amendment. During the floor vote, Feingold raised three of his proposed amendments, each of which was soundly and quickly defeated. Senate leaders feared that allowing one amendment to pass would lead to the unraveling of the agreement that Leahy had negotiated with the White House. The manager's amendment was a series of technical and other small changes that Senate leaders in consultation with the White House had agreed. However, when this amendment made it to the floor, Sen. Hatch delayed it, and this delay, in the end, killed the amendment. Democrats were furious, since they had negotiated the amendment with the White House. In the end, late on October 11, 2001, the Senate passed the USA Act on a 98–1 vote (Howell 2004, 1145–1207). The bill had been so quickly put together and negotiated that many who voted for it never saw a complete version of the final bill.

The House process worked differently, primarily because the civil liberties coalition succeeded in persuading Representative Bob Barr (R-GA) and four other Republican members of the House Judiciary Committee that Ashcroft's legislation went too far in expanding federal powers and infringing on individual rights. This resulted in the five Republicans writing a letter to Rep. Sensenbrenner, the committee chair, demanding time to make changes to the bill and to allow more public input into its development. Sensenbrenner received the letter on Friday, September 21, two days after Ashcroft and Leahy presented their bills to the public. On Monday, September 24, Sensenbrenner's committee held a public hearing with Ashcroft in attendance. Ashcroft, however, spent little time in addressing the committee, and allowed only thirty minutes of questions. Sensenbrenner had hoped that he could move the bill through his committee on September 25, but coupled with the letter and Democratic anger after the short hearing on September 24, Sensenbrenner knew that he would not be able to obtain the needed number of votes. The result was that the committee began to formally consider and markup the bill. The process was pushed much quicker than normal, but in the end, the Provide Appropriate Tools Required to Intercept and Obstruct Terrorism Act (PATRIOT ACT) emerged after one week and it was quite different than the one proposed by Ashcroft. It also passed the committee unanimously by a vote of 36–0 (Brill 2003).

The most important change that Sensenbrenner's committee made to Ashcroft's proposal was to sunset the most controversial aspects of the bill. This means that a change would be allowed only for a few years and then would have to be re-authorized by Congress. Failure to gain re-authorization would mean that the provision lapsed and the executive branch would no longer have the authority to continue the action. The period of authority was also short—two years. The House wanted Congress to have the chance to rapidly reexamine the new powers given to the executive branch and assess their effects on individual liberties and the ability to fight terrorism (Brill 2003).

Ashcroft and President Bush were not happy with the bill that emerged from Sensenbrenner's committee. They especially opposed the sunset provisions that had been added to it. Between October 2, the day Sensenbrenner's committee approved the bill, and October 12, Ashcroft worked to force changes to the bill. His work paid off as early as on the morning of October 12, Ashcroft persuaded then Speaker of the House, Dennis Hastert (R-IL), to accept the Senate version of the terrorism bill and substitute it for Sensenbrenner's bill (Brill 2003). When Sensenbrenner's bill was brought to the floor of the House later that same day for action, the House leadership offered an amendment substituting new language for the entire bill. The amendment was accepted. A motion was then made to send the amended bill back to Sensenbrenner's committee for review. This motion failed 73–345. The failure allowed the House to then vote on the bill, and it passed 337–79 (Howell 2004, 1145–1207).

The only things that remained from Sensenbrenner's original PATRIOT Act were the House bill number, a few small sections of the original bill that had been added to the Senate version of the bill, and most significantly the sunsets for many of the surveillance measures. To make them more palatable for the president and Ashcroft, the House leadership had extended them from two years to five years.

As in the Senate, many members who voted for the bill never saw the complete text. They were informed of the substitute language as they were voting for it on the morning of October 12. Opponents in the House expressed dismay that a bill as far reaching as the PATRIOT Act could be passed without members knowing what was in it, and that for the first time in the history of the House, a piece of legislation that changed criminal procedure and was related to constitutional rights was passed without having gone through the judiciary committee for review first (Brill 2003).

The passage of the House bill did not end the legislative process. The Constitution requires that for a bill to become a law both the House and Senate must pass it in exactly the same form. The bills that passed on October 11 and 12 in the Senate and House were close but not duplicates. It would take another two weeks for negotiators for the House and Senate to iron out the differences in the bill. Normally, a conference committee is created to do this. However, the House refused to create one. Beryl Howell, a committee staffer for Leahy's Senate Judiciary Committee and an author of an article examining the making of the USA PATRIOT Act, believes that the House's decision was very likely driven by the White House. The White House feared that a conference committee would empower the critics of the law since its members would have been drawn from the leadership of the judiciary committees from both houses. Thus, Sensenbrenner and Congressman John Conyers (D-MI) from the House would have been members, along with Leahy and Hatch from the Senate. Hatch would have been outnumbered three to one, and a bill looking much like Sensenbrenner's original may have emerged. By not agreeing to a conference committee, the House changed the normal dynamics of negotiating the final bill.

Senate and House leaders worked without a formal committee structure to fashion a final agreement. At the same time, a new set of terror attacks began in the United States. Anthrax was mailed to a variety of members of the House and Senate starting on October 15. This led to the closing of the Capitol for days, making negotiation difficult. On October 23, the House leadership unilaterally ended negotiations with the Senate, and submitted to the House a new Uniting and Strengthening America by Providing Appropriate Tools Required to Intercept and Obstruct Terrorism Act (USA PATRIOT Act). Senate negotiators were angry about this activity but could do nothing. The following day, Sensenbrenner asked the House to pass the new bill without amendment, so that it could be sent on to the Senate for approval. After some questioning and debate, the new bill passed 357–66.

The Senate was now pressured to pass the House version of the negotiated bill. Amending the bill would force more negotiations and delay, and these would then be blamed on the Senate and in particular the Democrats in the Senate who controlled it. Not wishing to pay these political costs, the Senate leadership brought the House USA PATRIOT Act to the floor of the Senate on October 25 where it passed on a 99–1 vote. President George Bush signed it into law the next day.

A BRIEF SUMMARY OF THE USA PATRIOT ACT

The USA PATRIOT ACT is over 130 pages long and contains more than one thousand sections. However, its contents can be summarized under several broad headings.[5] Details on the most important or controversial parts of the law are given in this section, as well as a list of other less significant parts of the law.

First, the law significantly enhanced the ability of government agents to track and surveil. Prior to the PATRIOT Act, a court order was needed in each jurisdiction for pen register and trap and trace devices. These devices allow agents to capture the metadata of phone calls, and now e-mails. This means that an agent knows who is communicating, when, how long, and where. Agents are not allowed to see the content of the communications unless a warrant has been obtained. While agents cannot use pen register devices without court certification, probable cause does not need to be established by them to gain certification. The agents must merely tell a court that the device is needed in an investigation and the court must then approve the use of the device (Howell 2004, 1145–1207).

The USA PATRIOT Act also made it easier for federal agents to access business records. The FBI has been allowed to issue "National Security Letters" (NSL) for several decades. These are in essence subpoenas that require no court order, and allow the FBI to demand customer records from a variety of businesses. The information that can be accessed includes the names of customers, their addresses, merchandise purchased, etc. The USA PATRIOT Act made it easier and quicker for the FBI to issue NSLs by eliminating the need for agents to obtain permission from FBI headquarters. Special agents in charge of a field office now have the authority to grant NSLs. Agents also no longer needed to show that the focus of an NSL was a foreign agent or someone connected to a foreign agent. It can now be sought if it was needed to protect against international terrorism or clandestine activity (Doyle 2011).

Prior to the USA PATRIOT Act, if the FBI needed greater access to business records, it could ask for a FISA court order to obtain them. However, the FBI then needed to show that those records pertained to a foreign power or agent, and that the records were relevant to an investigation. Also, only four types of businesses could be targeted. Section 215 of the USA PATRIOT Act eliminated the first requirement, eased the second by requiring the information to be related to an investigation of a foreign power or agent, and allowed the FBI to request any records or tangible things that were needed in an investigation of terrorism or espionage. This language meant that any record at any business or organization in the United States could be accessed with a FISA court order. The law also prohibits a party receiving a National Security Letter, or a FISA court order, from disclosing its receipt. This included disclosing the letter or order to an attorney if the party believes that the order was outside the scope of the law, or too broad in its reach (Gorham-Oscilowski and Jaeger 2008, 625–44). One limit was placed on the use of FISA orders to obtain business records. No order could be issued if it was motivated by the use of speech protected by the first amendment (Howell 2004, 1145–1207).

Prior to 9/11, the FBI interpreted the 1978 FISA Act as creating a wall between criminal investigations and intelligence investigations. Thus, an agent working to uncover a spy ring or other forms of espionage could not share information with agents working criminal cases, and vice versa. One reason for this wall is that the 1978 FISA Act created a means for the

FBI to obtain permission to wiretap in intelligence cases that had a lower burden of proof than those in criminal cases. In order to insure that a criminal case was not derailed through use of the weaker espionage standard, the FBI completely separated the two types of cases and prohibited the sharing of information by those involved in them. The USA PATRIOT Act changed that. It specifically calls for criminal and intelligence investigators to share information and allows them to work together (Bulzomi 2003, 25-32). Worrisome, for many, is that Congress also made it easier for FBI agents to obtain FISA wiretapping authority by changing the law from having intelligence gathering be the primary purpose for a warrant to a significant purpose of a warrant. This weaker condition opens the door for the FBI to use the FISA procedure to obtain wiretap warrants in criminal cases, instead of the much stricter probable cause requirement demanded by the Fourth Amendment.

A fourth change was to clarify and ease the ability of agents to perform sneak and peek searches. These are searches of a person's property without his or her awareness. The searches require a warrant, and for agents to actually seize evidence during a search, they must have proven the necessity of the seizure to the court issuing the warrant (Howell 2004, 1145–1207).

A fifth important change dealt with the handling of aliens and foreign students. The attorney general was authorized to detain and deport aliens suspected of involvement in terrorism, or who "may pose a threat to national security" (Connecticut General Assembly Office of Legislative Research 2001). Aliens can be detained for seven days without charge. After seven days, they must be released or the attorney general must begin deportation proceedings against them. An alien can be detained for an unlimited duration, if the person cannot be deported, but she is still considered a threat. In this case, an alien can ask for judicial review of the detention and seek to be released (Howell 2004, 1145–1207). The act also required the full implementation of a tracking system for foreign students in the United States (Doyle 2002).

Other parts of the law dealt with money laundering, counterfeiting, terrorism using biological weapons, terrorism directed at mass transit systems, material support to terrorists or terror groups, credit card fraud, and cyber crimes. The USA PATRIOT Act also extended the statute of limitations for terrorism crimes, changed the penalties for terrorism crimes, and made it easier for the federal government to assist states and municipalities after a terror attack (Doyle 2002). Finally, sunsets were created for the most controversial sections of the bill, those dealing with surveillance, wiretapping, and the collection of business records. All of these items would have to be re-authorized in 2005, or they would disappear.

GARBAGE CANS AND THE USA PATRIOT ACT

Earlier, the discussion of Kingdon's model of policymaking showed how the problem, policy, and politics streams combine to move issues onto the agenda and eventually lead to the formation of new law. The discussion of the passage of the USA PATRIOT Act illuminates the streams and their convergence quite well.

Terrorism was not a new problem or issue. However, it appears that for many policymakers, the changes to the terrorism laws after the 1995 Oklahoma City bombing had "solved" the issue. The reforms made then had improved security enough that no new legislation was required. To some extent, this can be seen in the ignoring of various reports and commissions on U.S. vulnerabilities to terrorism published between 1995 and 2001. During this period, the U.S. government commissioned five reports from three commissions on terrorism. Two commissions also delivered reports after the 9/11 attacks. However, none of the reports prior to 9/11 led to any serious legislative action in Congress, or a push from the executive branch for policy changes, despite the strong warnings given by the reports. For instance, the first Hart-Rudman report published in 1999 warned that the United States "will become increasingly vulnerable to hostile attacks in our homeland and that our military superiority will not entirely protect us." It went on to warn that "'Americans will likely die on American soil, possibly in large numbers'" (qtd. in Ball 2004, 25). The Bush administration tabled the Hart-Rudman report after a meeting in mid-2001. After the 9/11 attacks, Rudman was quoted as saying, "'We tend not to do what we ought to do until we get hit between the eyes'" (qtd. in Ball 2004, 27).

Not only may the issue have been seen as solved, the president was faced with other more urgent issues. In the first year of George W. Bush's administration, he had to deal with a downed spy plane in China, changes to the relationship with the Russians, and the collapse of the peace process in the Middle East (National Commission on the Terrorist Attacks Upon the United States 2004).

Also, it is clear from the 9/11 Commission Report that the president framed the terror problem in a way that prevented precautions from being taken in the United States, or asking for new legislation. For example, the administration debated aiding the Northern Alliance in Afghanistan as a way to check Al Qaeda, and worked to examine how a group like Al Qaeda might obtain weapons of mass destruction overseas. Terrorism was a threat, but it was a foreign threat, not a domestic one. And it was seen by many in government as more of a nuisance than catastrophic.

One school of thought, Clarke wrote in this September 4 note, implicitly argued that the terrorist network was a nuisance that killed a score of Americans every eighteen to twenty-four months. If that view was credited, then current policies might be proportionate. Another school saw Al Qaeda as the "point of the spear of radical Islam." But no one forced the argument into the open by calling for a national estimate or a broader discussion of the threat. The issue was never joined as collective debate by the U.S. Government, including the Congress, before 9/11 (National Commission on the Terrorist Attacks Upon the United States 2004, 343).

This quote shows clearly that how an issue is framed affects whether policy gets passed or whether an issue rises onto the agenda. Those who saw Al Qaeda as a domestic threat were not able to get their arguments heard, and thus the issue stayed off the agenda. Hence, it took a focusing event to bring terrorism back onto the legislative and policymaking agenda. In this case, the catastrophe of 9/11.

One can also clearly see the solution stream in the discussion of the passage of the USA PATRIOT Act. Remember, Kingdon argues that there are solutions waiting to be connected to a problem. If the time becomes right, a person supporting a solution or solutions will seek to connect them to the problem, whether they are a particularly good fit or not.

In the weeks between 9/11 and the passage of the USA PATRIOT Act, no systematic study was performed on the weaknesses or vulnerabilities that allowed the attack. Some information was quickly available that aircraft and airport security was lax, and that agencies within the federal government needed to communicate better. However, much of what entered the USA PATRIOT Act had no relation to the attacks. Instead, a variety of solutions that individuals could plausibly argue would help deter or prevent terrorism ended up incorporated into the bill.

Recall that Viet Dinh, the Deputy Attorney General, headed a meeting on September 12 where he asked U.S. attorneys and other top staff in the Department of Justice to suggest legislative reforms to deter and prevent terrorism. Within eight days, Dinh had enough material for a 40-page legislative proposal. Many of the ideas in that proposal had been around for years, and some of them had failed to become policy in 1996 when Congress refused to pass them as part of the legislation that came after the Oklahoma City bombing (Brill 2003; Kassop 2003, 509–29). September 11 gave supporters of these old ideas a new chance to get them enacted into law, and many of them were.

It was not just executive branch personnel that connected pet solutions or desired solutions to the USA PATRIOT Act. Sen. Leahy, in crafting the USA Act, drew on work completed by the Senate Banking Committee on money laundering. While Ashcroft's proposed legislation included a section dealing with money laundering, Leahy's bill was much more comprehensive, and most of what he proposed was enacted into legislation. It is for this reason that we see things like changes to the law dealing with counterfeiting and international credit card fraud in the USA PATRIOT Act. It is not because Al Qaeda used these things in executing 9/11; it is because Sen. Leahy could draw on a complete set of proposals from a Senate committee, and it could be easily argued that targeting the finances of groups could prevent future acts of terror.

The politics stream can also be seen. First, in order to speed passage of the act, the number of people involved in the process was limited. The Senate never sent the bill to committee for markup or a vote. Instead, Sen. Leahy and a few others worked with Ashcroft and his advisors on the bill. In the House, the bill did go to committee. But, in the end, the bill that was voted on was negotiated between the Speaker of the House and Ashcroft. Finally, even during reconciliation, no committee was formed. Instead, leaders of the House and Senate negotiated directly and informally to create one law that could pass both houses of Congress.

The 9/11 Committee report also remarks upon how changes in personnel between the Clinton Administration and the Bush Administration led to changes in how terrorism was perceived and reported. Richard Clarke, head of the Counter-terrorism Study Group in the White House, saw his access to principle policymakers changed and curtailed when Bush became president. This was not because Bush saw him as less valuable; it was because Bush had a different view on how organizations should run than Clinton, and his view led him to require groups like Clarke's to report through deputies, not directly to cabinet level officials. Clarke's lack of access to the president helped prevent his views on the terror threat from being heard.

The public mood also affected what was possible. The media largely ignored the various commission reports published between 1996 and 2001. Terrorism was not considered that large of a threat. The *New York Times* even questioned in a 1999 article whether Osama Bin Laden was really involved in the terror acts attributed to him by the U.S. government (National Commission on the Terrorist Attacks Upon the United States 2004). However, after the attacks, the mood of the media radically changed. One study found that media coverage echoed some of the major themes of the Bush Administration during the weeks the USA PATRIOT Act was being fashioned, particularly the ideas that time was of the essence, and that Congress needed to act (Domke et al. 2006, 291–312). In doing so, it created a sense of urgency that helped push Congress to act faster than it may have wanted. It also prevented opponents of legislation from using delay as a tactic to force changes or kill the proposals.

Prior to 9/11, the lack of media interest is partly attributable to a lack of public interest in the issue as well. Gallup began asking a question about how worried a person was that someone in his or her family would be a victim of terrorism in 1995 as a result of the Oklahoma City bombing. The percent of people reporting they were very or somewhat worried fell from 42 percent in 1995 to 24 percent in 2000. Only 4 percent of respondents were very worried that a family member would be a victim in 2000 (Gallup 2013). The marginality of the issue is also shown by Pew Research Center for the Public and the Press not beginning to ask a question on whether terrorism should be a national priority until 2002 (Pew Research Center for the People and the Press 2012).

However, once 9/11 occurred, the public mood swung quickly in a direction that would support policy change. In a Gallup poll performed the first week of October 2001, 59 percent of Americans were very worried or somewhat worried that a person in their family would be a victim of terrorism, more than double the level of concern a year earlier. Eighty-three percent of Americans also stated that it was somewhat or very likely that further terror attacks would occur over the next several weeks.

Americans also supported the idea of giving up some civil liberties in order to gain security. Pew Research Center for the People and the Press found that in mid-September 2001, 55 percent of Americans believed that giving up some civil liberties was necessary. This was up from 29 percent in April 1997, the last time the question had been asked. Majority support for giving up some liberties was found again in a poll conducted in January 2002 (Pew Research Center for the People and the Press 2011, 19). Such attitudes made it easier to expand federal government surveillance powers in the USA PATRIOT Act and helped supporters of the act overcome opponents.

THE USA PATRIOT ACT IN ACTION

Assessing the impact and implementation of the USA PATRIOT Act is difficult due to the complexity of the act, and its designed purpose to deter and prevent terrorism. How does one determine if a law deterred or prevented terrorism? An act prevented or not committed is immeasurable and therefore cannot be seen. Also, considering the space limits for this chapter, it is impossible to examine all parts of the implementation of the law. With these two items in mind, this section of the chapter will examine the implementation of the most controversial sections of the USA PATRIOT Act, those dealing with expanded federal authority to surveil inside the United States.

In the summary of the act, it was noted that Congress made it easier for the FBI to issue National Security Letters (NSLs) and to obtain FISA warrants to wiretap. These changes have had a large impact on the FBI's willingness to use these tools. Data from the Electronic Privacy Information Center show that the number of NSLs concerning U.S. citizens has skyrocketed since 2004, going from 8,943 to 15,229 in 2012.[6] In 2008 and 2010, the number of NSLs served were over 24,000 each year. These numbers are low estimates of the number of people and requests made through NSLs. The Inspector General's Office of the Department of Justice reported in 2007 that many NSLs contain multiple information requests (DOJ 2007 report). Thus, a letter may ask a telephone company for information from multiple phone numbers and people. The DOJ 2007 report concluded that between 2003 and 2005, 44,000 NSLs were served and these letters made more than 136,000 information requests.

Not only has the use of NSLs skyrocketed since the passage of the USA PATRIOT Act, but also there has been a shift in their focus from non-U.S. citizens to U.S. citizens. The DOJ Inspector General found that in 2003 39 percent of NSL requests dealt with a U.S. citizen. By 2005, this had increased to 53 percent (United States Department of Justice 2007). This further increased to 57 percent in 2006 (United States Department of Justice 2008). Data do not exist to show these trends beyond 2006. While the FBI reports annually to Congress the number of NSLs that requested information on U.S. citizens, it does not report what percent of all requests deal with Americans. The trends are only reported in the two inspector generals' reports that resulted from an investigation of FBI issuance and use of NSLs.

Besides noting the trends in NSL use, the DOJ Inspector General reports were also very critical of the FBI. They found that the FBI failed to properly record NSL issuance, it had occasionally made unacceptably broad NSL requests, it had received information from NSLs that it was not entitled to receive, and that it had issued NSLs without meeting even the weaker standard created by the USA PATRIOT Act (United States Department of Justice 2008). The report also noted that the FBI was issuing NSLs to collect information on individuals that were associated beyond arms length with others in an investigation. These individuals were often separated by more than two persons from the initial subject of an investigation (Gorham-Oscilowski and Jaeger 2008, 625–44). The FBI responded to the first DOJ Inspector General report by creating new standards for FBI offices to follow and mandating extra training for agents on NSLs.

Two court cases dealing with NSL requests have been heard since passage of the USA PATRIOT Act. The first case arose from an internet service provider (ISP) challenging the constitutionality of the section of the PATRIOT Act that prevents disclosure of an NSL forever, and because the act offers no ability for judicial review. The court ruled in favor of the ISP, agreeing that the inability to challenge an NSL in court violated the Fourth Amendment, and that the requirement that an NSL be kept secret in perpetuity violated the First Amendment. The court stated that secrecy could be demanded, but that at some point, the reasons for secrecy end, and thus disclosure cannot be prohibited after that point.

The second case was brought by a group of libraries in Connecticut that had received an NSL allowing the FBI to have all information pertaining to a specific computer during a period of time. Again, the disclosure requirement was challenged, and again the court ruled that the USA PATRIOT Act went too far in preventing speech. The non-disclosure requirements were so strict that unnamed plaintiffs initially filed the cases.

It was only after the government conceded the cases that the names of those involved were exposed (Gorham-Oscilowski and Jaeger 2008, 625–44).

In reaction to these two cases, Congress in re-authorizing the USA PATRIOT Act in 2005 changed the disclosure requirements of the law. Individuals or companies receiving an NSL were given explicit permission within the law to challenge it in the court system. Also, while an entity receiving an NSL could not disclose it, Congress did allow the entity to discuss it with legal counsel. Finally, the amendments provided a process and method of review to lift the non-disclosure requirement of an NSL. Thus, NSLs would no longer remain secret forever.

More controversial has been the use of Section 215 powers by the FBI and the National Security Agency. This is the section that allows the government to collect business records or any tangible things needed in an intelligence or espionage investigation.

In June 2013, the *Guardian* reported that Verizon had been ordered by the Foreign Intelligence Surveillance Court to provide the FBI and NSA "on an 'ongoing, daily, basis'" access to millions of customers' call data during the period from April 19 to July 19, 2013. The information included the numbers called, duration of each call, telephone calling card numbers, and other routing and call identifiers. Customer records turned over dealt both with calls made from the United States to outside locations as well as calls that were completely inside the United States. The FISA court ruled that section 215 of the USA PATRIOT Act authorized the bulk collection of business records if they could be shown to have a tangible use in the prevention of terrorism (Greenwald 2013).

The day after the story broke, the Obama administration confirmed the story and admitted that the FBI and NSA had been collecting the metadata from telephone and internet companies for years. Senator Dianne Feinstein (D-CA) stated that the order was just a renewal of what had been going on for the last seven years. Congressman Sensenbrenner, one of the lead participants in creating the USA PATRIOT Act, stated that "'I do not believe the broadly drafted FISA order is consistent with the requirements of the PATRIOT Act. Seizing phone records of millions of innocent people is excessive and un-American'" (qtd. in Roberts and Ackerman 2013).

The *Guardian* story exposed in detail what two Democratic senators, Mark Udall and Ron Wyden, had been vaguely warning about for several years. Both senators sit on the Senate Intelligence Committee where they received classified briefings on FBI and NSA actions authorized by the USA PATRIOT Act. Because the briefings are secret, neither senator could publically discuss their details. However, they could allude to the briefings and discuss the fears stemming from them. During the debate in May 2011 to re-authorize the surveillance powers of the USA PATRIOT Act for second time, Sen. Wyden remarked that "I want to deliver a warning this afternoon: When the American People find out how their government has secretly interpreted the PATRIOT Act, they will be stunned and they will be angry" (qtd. in Savage 2011, A17).

A year later (March 15, 2012), Sens. Wyden and Udall wrote a letter to Attorney General Eric Holder criticizing the Obama administration's interpretation of the USA PATRIOT Act and especially section 215 (the business records provision). In the letter, Wyden and Udall stated:

> It is a matter of public record that section 215, which is a public statute, has been the subject of secret legal interpretations. . . . We believe that most Americans would be stunned to learn the details of how these secret court opinions have interpreted section 215 of the Patriot Act. As we see it, there is now a significant gap between what most Americans *think* the law allows and what the government *secretly claims* [emphasis in original] the law allows.... Americans know that their government will sometimes conduct secret operations, but they don't think that government officials should be writing secret law. (Udall and Wyden 2012)

They went on to request that the administration release the interpretations of the USA PATRIOT Act so that a proper debate over the powers given to the FBI and NSA could take place and for Americans to understand what the laws passed by the government mean.

After the *Guardian* story, Wyden, Udall and twenty-four other senators from both parties sent James Clapper, the Director of National Intelligence (DNI), a letter criticizing the bulk collection of phone records, and demanding the answer to a series of questions regarding the use of Section 215. The letter noted that:

> The bulk collection and aggregation of American's phone records has a significant impact on Americans' privacy that exceeds the issues considered by the Supreme Court in *Smith v. Maryland*[7] . . . These records can reveal personal relationships, family medical issues, political and religious affiliations, and a variety of other private personal information. This is particularly true if these records are collected in a manner that includes cell phone locational data, effectively turning Americans' cell phones into tracking devices. (Wyden et al. 2013)

The authors went on to express their concern that other types of records could also be seized by the FBI and NSA, including medical records, financial records, gun ownership records, etc. They remarked that while the Obama administration claimed that strict controls over access to the data were in place, that historically intelligence agencies had not always properly protected access to or the use of data. The authors then asked (1) how long bulk collection of telephone data had been occurring, (2) whether other forms of data were being collected, (3) whether cell phone location data had been collected, (4) whether any of the court orders allowing collection had been violated, (5) what specific acts of terrorism had been prevented or stopped by the bulk collection of data, (6) whether the data collected gave unique intelligence insights, and (7) what personnel had access to the data and whether they are federal employees or contractors.[8]

In the days that followed, it became clear that the NSA was collecting billions of records a day, not millions. The NSA claimed that the collection of records had helped to prevent at least 50 terror attacks, 10 domestic, and went on to expose one incident where call logs provided by the phone companies led to the prosecution and conviction of individuals materially supporting Al Shabab, a terror group based in Somalia. The individuals had raised $8,500 to be sent to the group (Savage 2013). The NSA was also shown to have made significant errors in its collection and accessing of records, and that the FISA court ruled in 2009 that some of the NSA's actions violated U.S. law. The FISA court in its 2009 opinion went so far as to state that the regime used to govern the collection and searching of bulk business records had never worked correctly (Savage and Shane 2013).

Director Clapper was also exposed as lying to Congress during hearings in March 2013. At those hearings, Clapper was asked if the NSA was collecting private information on millions of citizens. He stated that the NSA was not. In a June 21, 2013, letter to Sen. Feinstein, chair of the Senate Intelligence Committee, Clapper apologized for lying to Congress, but that he had made the "least untruthful" statement to protect the classified program (Shane and Weisman 2013).

Finally, it became clear that secret interpretations of the USA PATRIOT Act had authorized the bulk collection program. Government lawyers had argued before the court that "relevant" records under section 215 meant that all records could be accessed and stored for future use by investigators because they might be relevant at a future date (Granick and Sprigman 2013). The court agreed with this interpretation.

While many representatives and senators were alarmed by the news reports on domestic surveillance, the House and Senate Leadership were supportive of the program. Sen. Reid, now the Senate Majority Leader, and now Speaker Boehner both stated that the programs were "authorized by law and rigorously overseen by Congress and the courts" (quoted in Shane and Weisman 2013). Reid went further by stating that: "For senators to complain that they didn't know this was happening, we had many, many meetings that have been both classified and unclassified that members have been invited to. They shouldn't come and say, 'I wasn't aware of this,' because they've had every opportunity" (qtd. in Shane and Weisman 2013). The leaders of the House Intelligence Committee, Mike Rogers (R-MI) and C.A. "Dutch" Ruppersberger (D-MD) also publically supported the program. Rep. Rogers invited General Keith B. Alexander, head of the NSA, to a hearing on June 17 to explain how the programs had helped prevent terror in the United States (Savage 2013). The hearing was designed to bolster support for the program, not to criticize it.

A Q Poll released on July 10, 2013, showed that the public was largely supportive of the NSA programs, but also a bit worried about government going too far in regards to liberty and privacy. The poll specifically asked whether the respondents supported the scanning of all phone calls to see if they were linked to terrorism. Fifty-one percent of the sample said they supported the program. When asked if the scanning of phone calls was needed to keep Americans safe, 54 percent said yes. However, when asked if the program intruded too much into Americans' privacy, 53 percent said yes. Forty-five percent of respondents also answered that the government had gone too far in restricting the average person's civil liberties. This was up from 25 percent when the question was last asked in 2010. The poll also found that 55 percent of respondents thought that Edward Snowden was a whistleblower, not a traitor for exposing the various FBI and NSA data collection programs (Quinnipiac University Poll 2013).

Finally, the news reports led to the filing of at least three lawsuits challenging the bulk collection programs. The lawsuits were filed by the American Civil Liberties Union (ACLU), the Electronic Privacy Information Center (EPIC), and a coalition of nineteen groups led by the Electronic Frontier Foundation. The ACLU filed its case in the federal district court of New York on behalf of the customers of Verizon. EPIC said it would attempt to take its case directly to the Supreme Court. The reason for this unusual step is that its case will challenge rulings made by the FISA court, and since EPIC cannot argue in front of the FISA court, it has no recourse but to go directly to the Supreme Court. The third group filed suit in federal district court against the NSA. The coalition is a diverse one including gun-rights groups, civil liberties group, and a Unitarian church. All of the cases challenge the interpretations of the USA PATRIOT Act authorizing the bulk collection of calls and other business data of American citizens (Risen 2013b).

At the time this chapter was written, the debate and controversy surrounding the NSA program was swirling. In 2005, two court cases led to small amendments to the USA PATRIOT Act when the surveillance sections were reauthorized for the first time. In 2011, when the sections were reauthorized for the second time, no changes were made to the law. The extent of this controversy is likely to lead to far more debate when the act comes up for reauthorization for the third time in June 2015, and it is possible that Congress makes significant changes to the law or perhaps allows the surveillance authority it granted to the executive branch in October, 2001, to lapse. These debates and warnings over reauthorization have already begun. During a House Judiciary Committee hearing on July 17, Chairman Sensenbrenner cut off the testimony of James Cole (a deputy attorney general) defending the NSA program, and stated, "unless you realize you've got a problem, that [USA PATRIOT Act] is not going to be renewed" (qtd. in Risen 2013a, A14). He went further in a letter to now Attorney General Eric Holder stating that Section 215 is an urgent tool and crucial to intelligence agencies, but if such abuses are not reined in, it will be very difficult to reauthorize these provisions when they sunset in 2015" (Sensenbrenner 2013).

CONCLUSION

So what does the USA PATRIOT Act say about the policymaking process in the United States? First, the act clearly shows that legislation is contingent on the intersection of problem, policy, and politics streams. How problems are framed and the interest that actors have in them determine whether they move up, down, or off the agenda. Terrorism between 1996 and 2001 was seen as a problem, but not something requiring new laws. It took 9/11, a focusing event, to move the issue upward in both the public's mind and in that of policymakers. Solutions sit waiting for a problem to solve. September 11 opened a window for those seeking to pass policies that had been rejected in the past, roving wiretap authority, for instance, and for policies that were in committee to go from proposals to actual legislation, new money laundering rules, for example. If one could show that a policy might help prevent or stop terrorism, it had a chance to be included in the USA PATRIOT Act. It made no difference whether the solution actually targeted something that helped cause 9/11 or not. Finally, who is involved in crafting a bill and the nation's mood are vital for determining its passage and its final form. President Bush and John Ashcroft largely succeeded in getting the bill they wanted because they kept the number of players involved quite small. Democrats in the Senate, in particular, were loath to overly delay or challenge the administration's proposal for fear that they would buck the public mood of fear and a desire for quick action.

This case study also shows that laws can end up being used and implemented in ways that no one expected. James Sensenbrenner, one of the leaders in the House who helped craft the USA PATRIOT Act, was surprised to discover that section 215 allowing the collection of business records in a terror investigation had been interpreted to allow the bulk collection of billions of average Americans' phone records. He expressly stated that this was never the intent of Congress.

The courts have also played an active role in determining how the USA PATRIOT Act is implemented and used by the executive branch. Two early court decisions forced Congress to amend the law placing restrictions on the length of non-disclosure of National Security Letters (NSLs), and allowing those presented an NSL and FISA business records order to discuss them with legal counsel. Without these amendments, sections of the law deemed unconstitutional at the district level most likely would have been found unconstitutional by the appellate courts and finally the Supreme Court. Also, the FISA court created in 1978 has been an important actor in ruling on executive branch arguments about what the USA PATRIOT Act means. It is these rulings that have permitted the NSA and FBI programs that collect and scan the metadata created by Americans when they use telephone and cell phones in the country. No one at the time the act was passed thought that the FISA court would be an active interpreter of the law.

Finally, this case shows that laws are not static. They change over time as they are interpreted and used, and Congress often revisits them when it becomes aware of problems or issues with them. The USA PATRIOT Act may be more dynamic than some laws because it had sunset provisions built into it, which forced Congress to reexamine it and re-authorize it twice, already, with a third time coming in the middle of 2015. Policymakers are quite aware of this dynamism and this is why they attempt to expose interpretations of laws, and offer new ones. What a word in a law is deemed to mean as we saw with "relevant" is the difference between allowing the NSA to capture phone records of many Americans or of only those where evidence can be provided that a threat exists.

NOTES

1. The group was an interesting mix including standard civil liberties groups like the American Civil Liberties Union to technology groups like the Electronic Frontier Foundation and conservative groups like the Eagle Forum (O'Harrow 2002).

2. This is a device that records the activities from a telephone line. It does not capture actual content of a call, only the numbers called and the calls received.

3. Sneak and peak searches are searches of a home, office, etc., where the suspect is not notified of the search and the search is performed while the suspect is absent. These searches were allowed by FISA as part of a foreign intelligence operation but not in criminal cases.

4. Markup is the process is committee by which members amend and change a piece of legislation.

5. For a more detailed summary of the act, see Connecticut General Assembly, Office of Legislative Research 2001; Doyle 2002.

6. Data on NSLs were not reported annually to Congress until 2004. Thus, it is impossible to know the number of NSLs issued prior to 2001 with U.S. citizens involved. Considering the strong upward trend since 2004, and the more stringent requirements to obtain one, it is most likely that NSLs involving U.S. citizens were far lower prior to 9/11.

7. *Smith v. Maryland* (1979) was a Supreme Court case that determined that pen registers, a filter that allows law enforcement to monitor what numbers are called by a telephone, do not require a search warrant and do not violate the Fourth Amendment. The court's opinion was that because calls go through a third party, the phone company, a person does not have an expectation of privacy concerning the metadata created by the call. Content of conversations is protected, not the information concerning numbers called, the duration of calls, etc. The case is seen as allowing the same types of information collection from internet and cell phone companies by the FBI and NSA as part of Section 215 of the USA PATRIOT Act.

8. The final question was raised because the *Guardian* story exposing the massive data-gathering operation under Section 215 was based on information furnished to the paper by Edward Snowden, an employee of Booz, Allen, and Hamilton, a large intelligence contractor with the NSA (Borger 2013).

REFERENCES

Ball, Howard. 2004. *The USA PATRIOT ACT of 2001: Balancing Civil Liberties and National Security: A Reference Handbook*. Santa Barbara: ABC-CLIO, Inc.

Borger, Julian. 2013. "Booz Allen Hamilton: Edward Snowden's US Contracting Firm." *Guardian*, June 9. Accessed July 16, 2013. www.guardian.co.uk/world/2013/jun/09/booz-allen-hamilton-edward-snowden.

Brill, Steven. 2003. *After: How America Confronted the September 12 Era*. New York: Simon and Schuster.

Bulzomi, Michael J. 2003. "Foreign Intelligence Surveillance Act." *FBI Law Enforcement Bulletin* 72:25-32. Accessed July 15, 2013. http://www.fbi.gov/stats-services/publications/law-enforcement-bulletin/2003-pdfs/june03leb.pdf.

Connecticut General Assembly Office of Legislative Research. 2001. Summary of Federal "USA Patriot Act." Connecticut: Office of Legislative Research.

Domke, David, Erica S. Graham, Kevin Coe, Sue Lockett John, and Ted Coopman. 2006. "Going Public as Political Strategy: The Bush Administration, an Echoing Press, and Passage of the Patriot Act." *Political Communication* 23: 291–312.

Doyle, Charles. 2002. "The USA PATRIOT Act: A Sketch." Washington D.C.: Congressional Research Service, April 18. Accessed July 3, 2013. http://www.fas.org/irp/crs/RS21203.pdf.

Doyle, Charles. 2011. "National Security Letters: Proposals in the 112th Congress." Washington D.C.: Congressional Research Service, December 12. Accessed July 3, 2013. http://www.fas.org/sgp/crs/intel/RS22406.pdf.

Gallup. 2013. "Terrorism in the United States." Accessed July 12, 2013. http://www.gallup.com/poll/4909/terrorism-united-states.aspx.

Gorham-Oscilowski, Ursula, and Paul T. Jaeger. 2008. "National Security Letters, the USA Patriot Act, and the Constitution: The Tensions between National Security and Civil Rights." *Government Information Quarterly* 25: 625–44.

Granick, Jennifer Stisa, and Christopher Jon Sprigman. 2013. "The Criminal NSA." *New York Times*, June 27.

Greenwald, Glenn. 2013. "U.S. Orders Phone Firm to Hand Over Data on Millions of Calls: Top Secret Court Ruling Demands 'Ongoing, Daily' data from Verizon." *Guardian*, June 6.

Howell, Beryl A. 2004. "Seven Weeks: The Making of the USA PATRIOT Act." *George Washington Law Review* 72: 1145–1207.

Johnston, William Robert. 2013. "Terrorist attacks and related incidents in the United States." Accessed August 29, 2013. www.johnstonsarchive.net/terrorism/wrjp255a.html.

Kassop, Nancy. 2003. "The War Power and Its Limits." *Presidential Studies Quarterly* 33: 509–29.

Kingdon, John. 1990. *Agendas, Alternatives, and Public Policies*. New York: HarperCollins.

National Commission on the Terrorist Attacks Upon the United States. 2004. *The 9/11 Commission Report: Final Report of the National Commission on the Terrorist Attacks Upon the United States*. New York: W. W. Norton and Company, Inc.

O'Harrow, Robert Jr. 2002. "Six Weeks in Autumn." *Washington Post*, October 27.

Pew Research Center for the People and the Press. 2011. "United in Remembrance, Divided Over Policies: Ten Years after 9/11." September 1. Accessed August 29, 2013. www.people-press.org/files/legacy-pdf/9-1-11%20Sept.%2011%20Release.pdf.

Pew Research Center for the People and the Press. 2012. "Public Priorities: Deficit Rising, Terrorism Slipping: Tough Stance on Iran Endorsed." January 23. Accessed August 29, 2013. www.people-press.org/files/legacy-pdf/1-23-12%20Priorities%20Release.pdf.

Quinnipiac University Poll. 2013. "U.S. Voters Say Snowden Is Whistle-Blower, Not Traitor, Quinnipiac University National Poll Finds; Big Shift On Civil Liberties vs. Counter-Terrorism." July 10. Accessed July 16, 2013. www.quinnipiac.edu/institutes-and-centers/polling-institute/national/release-detail?ReleaseID=1919.

Risen, James. 2013a. "Bipartisan Backlash Grows Against Domestic Surveillance." *New York Times*, July 18.

Risen, James. 2013b. "Privacy Group to Ask Supreme Court to Stop N.S.A.'s Phone Spying Program." *New York Times*, July 7.

Roberts, Dan, and Spencer Ackerman. 2013. "U.S. Admits Secret Surveillance of Phone Calls Has Gone On for Years: Anger Grows over Scale of Operation: Seized Data Vital for Security, Obama Says: Surveillance of Calls has Gone on for Years." *Guardian*, June 7.

Savage, Charlie. 2011. "Senators Say Patriot Act is Being Misinterpreted." *New York Times*, May 26.

Savage, Charlie. 2013. "N.S.A. Chief Says Surveillance Has Stopped Dozens of Plots." *New York Times*, June 18. Accessed July 16. www.nytimes.com/2013/06/19/us/politics/nsa-chief-says-surveillance-has-stopped-dozens-of-plots.html?ref=nationalsecurityagency.

Savage, Charlie, and Scott Shane. 2013. "Secret Court Rebuked N.S.A. on Surveillance." *New York Times*, August 21. Accessed August 29. www.nytimes.com/2013/08/22/us/2011-ruling-found-an-nsa-program-unconstitutional.html?pagewanted=all&_r=0.

Sensenbrenner, James. 2013. "Letter to Attorney General Eric Holder on the Over Broad Interpretation of the USA PATRIOT ACT." June 6. Accessed July 3, 2013. sensenbrenner.house.gov/uploadedfiles/sensenbrenner_letter_to_attorney_general_eric_holder.pdf.

Shane, Scott, and Weisman Jonathan. 2013. "Earlier Denials Put Intelligence Chief in Awkward Position." *New York Times*, June 11. Accessed July 16. www.nytimes.com/2013/06/12/us/nsa-disclosures-put-awkward-light-on-official-statements.html?ref=nationalsecurityagency.

Shenon, Philip. 2001. "Ashcroft Wants Quick Action on Broader Wiretapping Plan." *New York Times*, September 18. Accessed July 9, 2013. search.proquest.com/docview/431869183?accountid=13743.

Smith v. Maryland. 1979. 442 US 735. Accessed August 29, 2013. supreme.justia.com/cases/federal/us/442/735/case.html.

Templeton, Tom, and Tom Lumley. 2002. "9-11 in Numbers." *Guardian*, August 17. Accessed August 29, 2013. www.theguardian.com/world/2002/aug/18/usa.terrorism.

Udall, Mark, and Ron Wyden. 2012. "Letter to Eric Holder, Attorney General, on Seeking the Dismissal of Two Lawsuits under the Freedom of Information Act and the Problem of Secret Law." March 15. Accessed July 3, 2013. www.documentcloud.org/documents/325953-85512347-senators-ron-wyden-mark-udall-letter-to.html.

United States Department of Justice Office of the Inspector General. 2007. "A Review of the Federal Bureau of Investigation's Use of National Security Letters." United States Department of Justice. Accessed July 15, 2013. http://www.justice.gov/oig/special/s0703b/final.pdf.

United States Department of Justice Office of the Inspector General. 2008. "A Review of the FBI's Use of National Security Letters: Assessment of Corrective Actions and Examination of NSL Usage in 2006." United States Department of Justice. Accessed July 15, 2013. http://www.justice.gov/oig/special/s0803b/final.pdf.

Wyden, Ron, Mark Udall, Lisa Murkowski, Patrick Leahy, Mark Kirk, Dick Durbin, Tom Udall, Brian Schatz, Jon Tester, Jeanne Shaheen, Dean Heller, Mark Begich, Bernie Sanders, Patty Murray, Jeff Merkley, Mazie Hirono, Al Franken, Tom Harkin, Chris Coons, Maria Cantwell, Richard Blumenthal, Max Baucus, Elizabeth Warren, Martin Heinrich, Tammy Baldwin, and Mike Lee. 2013. "Letter to James R. Clapper, DNI, on Bulk Data Collection Program," June 27. Accessed July 3, 2013. http://www.fas.org/irp/congress/2013_cr/dni-bulk.pdf.

NINE

Evolving Lessons of Lawmaking in a Dynamic System

Robert Dewhirst and Sunil Ahuja

So just what do the authors of these seven case studies have to tell us about the nature of the policymaking process in the American system of government during the first decades of the twenty-first century? The answer is—a lot. Despite the numerous differences found in these seven policy endeavors, several important generalizations could be made about what these case studies reveal collectively—what they say about the American system and what they teach us about national policymaking in this new century. Overall, this was not a particularly productive legislative period in American history. However, some important measures did complete the often arduous journey through the legislative labyrinth from agenda appearance to adopted public policy.

DEEPLY DIVIDED POLICYMAKERS AND A DIVIDED ELECTORATE

First, perhaps the most powerful theme running throughout these case studies is the current deep division in American politics. The division is both partisan and ideological and courses through each of the three branches of government. The early years of the twenty-first century have been perhaps the most excessive time of hyperpartisanship in American political history. Scholars have produced thoughtful analysis of these developments. See in particular works by Geoffrey Kabaservice (2013) or Theda Skocpol and Vanessa Williamson (2013). To begin with, numerous major U.S. Supreme Court decisions commonly have been decided by the narrowest possible 5–4 verdict, punctuated with dissenting and concurring opinions on each side.

Nearby on Capitol Hill both chambers of Congress commonly were hamstrung with ideological divisions hampering unity among Republicans in the House of Representatives and partisan warfare more intense and commonplace than what has been seen in generations. This turmoil has been well examined by scholars. See, for example, studies by Sunil Ahuja (2008) or Thomas Mann and Norman Ornstein (2012). To be sure, often extraordinary efforts were required by numerous participants to win passage of the proposals sought here. Commonly sufficient agreement to allow the passage of legislation through both houses of Congress has been rare. More likely, the House passed legislation, such as repealing Obamacare, which was rejected by the Senate. Conversely, the Senate approved legislation that met with a "dead on arrival" pronouncement in the House.

In sum, President Barack Obama was confronted with an intense opposition political party, which only rarely was willing to compromise to pass any legislation or approve any nominee. Increasingly, the most intense Republican stalwarts on Capitol Hill refused to compromise on anything they believed to "a matter of principle." And they tended to vehemently oppose on principle almost anything proposed by the Democrats or President Obama.

More often than not, Congress was at a stalemate. Following their takeover after the 2010 elections, Republican majorities in the House of Representatives focused almost exclusively on passing nearly fifty measures seeking to repeal Obamacare. Meanwhile, Senate Republicans used their filibuster powers to bottleneck countless legislation and presidential appointments.

Each of the case studies in this book represents legislative victories where majorities against at times difficult odds were able to win passage of important legislation. To be sure, several of these measures were the product of American institutions responding to extreme pressures in a crisis environment such as a major terrorist attack or a massive and widespread economic downturn. On the other hand, one measure won ultimate approval following a long-term festering problem—healthcare.

In sum, on one hand, a crisis can elevate a problem to produce fairly quickly (by governmental standards) a proposed solution. On the other hand, a long festering problem (such as healthcare) can win passage via an unlikely and unusual array of circumstances unique to that issue and time.

TWO MAJOR BLOWS INFLICTED ON AMERICA

A second factor hovering over the era was ignited by two major catastrophic events which likely left political and economic scars on the public and will likely last for decades afterward—the murder of thousands of people stemming from a series of terrorist attacks of 2011 and the banking financial crisis of 2008 which triggered what quickly was termed the "Great Recession."

Terrorist Attacks

The terrorist attacks on New York City, the Pentagon, and a field in Pennsylvania on September 11, 2011, ignited a powerful public outcry and call for action. Congress responded with the passage of the USA PATRIOT Act of 2001 and the amendments in 2006 and 2011 as chronicled in chapter eight. The intensity of the debate challenged previous assumptions about guaranteeing defendants' rights, torture of prisoners, and Internet spying.

The Great Recession

The banking and financial crisis of 2008 triggered what was quickly dubbed "the Great Recession." Widespread corporate and personal bankruptcies became commonplace as countless Americans were thrown out of work, lost important benefits, or suffered significant income reduction. While there appeared little congressional agreement other than the nation confronted a major problem, legislators did manage to pass two major pieces of legislation—the Dodd-Frank Wall Street Reform and Consumer Protection Act of 2010 (chapter 6) and the American Taxpayer Relief Act of 2012.

Unfortunately, for numerous reasons, family income remained stagnant during this period despite the stock market rallying to beyond the 17,000 mark. Political malaise continued throughout the period, which was marred by a government shutdown and an unprecedented downgrading of the nation's credit rating. Fiscal confrontation became commonplace on Capitol Hill.

Combining the widespread loss of healthcare coverage by unemployed and underemployed Americans, President Obama and his Democratic allies on Capitol Hill won passage of perhaps the most significant piece of legislation during this period—the Patient Protection and Affordable Care Act of 2011. Quickly dubbed "Obamacare," the program was the most noteworthy domestic legislation since the passage of civil rights and Medicare and Medicaid legislation in the 1960s. One of the factors making this even more noteworthy was that it was passed during an intense and often bitter partisan period, while the previous bills passed in a time of Democratic partisan dominance.

OTHER FACTORS WEIGH IN

The Electorate Speaks

National elections also played a critical role in affecting American policymaking during this period. Fittingly enough, the period covered here was launched with a presidential election featuring the popular vote-winner, Al Gore, losing to the Electoral College vote-winner George W. Bush. Moreover, the winner hinged on the highly-disputed and controversial vote tally in Florida.

Indicative of the deep and narrow partisan divisions in the country, majority control of Congress changed hands more than once during this period. Heard almost everywhere were claims to voters that "control of the (House) or (Senate) hinges on the outcome of this race." With a nervous and worried electorate, such claims were not necessarily campaign hyperbole. At one time or another, each party enjoyed control of at least one chamber.

The Supreme Court Speaks

During this period, the U.S. Supreme Court continued its pattern of making seminal rulings on the back of narrow 5–4 majorities. Perhaps the seminal ruling was the 2010 verdict in *Citizens United v. FEC*. This ruling (chapter 6) crushed what little remained of the Bipartisan Campaign Reform Act and led to the virtually unfettered flow of campaign contributions from corporations and wealthy Americans. Of note here was the rapid expansion of ideologically-based interest group political action committees. Most, but certainly not all, of this activity came from conservative activists.

Important Domestic Policy Advances

Meanwhile, despite such a partisan environment, noteworthy domestic legislation managed to fight through the political headwinds and become law. The Lilly Ledbetter Fair Pay Act of 2009 (chapter 2), the first major domestic act signed by President Obama, helped women win a major employment equity advance. The Higher Education Opportunity Act of 2008 (chapter 5) focused on critical education needs. Finally, the Don't Ask, Don't Tell Repeal Act of 2010 (chapter 3) was an early step in the march toward equal rights for gay and lesbian citizens, which progressed throughout this period.

CONCLUSION

Overall, in a pluralistic and democratic society such as the United States, one fundamental message concerning policymaking has been that seldom is everyone totally happy with the end product of a policy. The built-in system of separation of powers and checks and balances has facilitated such policy outcomes. The time spanning the development of policies here was marked by the separation of powers/checks and balances during one of its shrillest periods. Yet, legislation managed to win passage nonetheless.

In sum, one wonders what James Madison and his colleagues would have thought about American national politics in the early decades of the twenty-first century.

REFERENCES

Ahuja, Sunil. 2008. *Congress Behaving Badly: The Rise of Partisanship and Incivility and the Death of Public Trust*. Westport, CT: Praeger.

Kabaservice, Geoffrey. 2013. *Rule and Ruin: The Downfall of Moderation and the Destruction of the Republican Party, From Eisenhower to the Tea Party*. New York: Oxford University Press.

Mann, Thomas E., and Norman J. Ornstein. 2012. *It's Even Worse Than It Looks: How The American Constitutional System Collided With The New Politics Of Extremism*. New York: Basic.

Skocpol, Theda, and Vanessa Williamson. 2013. *The Tea Party and the Remaking of Republican Conservatism*. New York: Oxford University Press.

Index

About the Contributors

Sunil Ahuja is vice president for accreditation relations, institutional change, and research at the Higher Learning Commission. He received his PhD in political science from the University of Nebraska in 1995. Dr. Ahuja is a former dean and a professor of political science. He has held faculty positions at Youngstown State University, Seton Hall University, and at the University of Louisiana at Lafayette. He has taught American Government, Congress, Presidency, Public Policy, and Research Methods, among other courses, and his research interests include political institutions, legislative politics, and congressional leadership.

Robert Dewhirst is professor of political science at Northwest Missouri State University. He received his PhD in political science from the University of Nebraska in 1983. Dr. Dewhirst's teaching and research cover American government and politics, state politics, Congress, the American presidency, campaigns and elections, media and politics, political parties, and public policy. He has published several books and numerous book chapters, articles, and essays in these areas.

Margaret E. Banyan is associate professor and MPA program coordinator at Florida Gulf Coast University. She received her PhD in public administration and policy from Portland State University. Dr. Banyan teaches in the Division of Public Affairs in the areas of land use planning, public administration, and political science. Her research interests include public participation, citizen engagement, civic capacity, cross-sectional partnerships and collaboration, and civic infrastructure development in urban, rural, and cross-cultural settings.

Peter J. Bergerson is professor of political science at Florida Gulf Coast University. He received his PhD in political science from Saint Louis University and has been a professor for over forty years, publishing several books and numerous articles as well as lecturing in Europe, the Middle East, and Asia. Dr. Bergerson's teaching and research interests include political institutions, campaigns and elections, public personnel administration, and leadership in public organizations.

Douglas M. Brattebo is associate professor and director of the James A. Garfield Center for the Study of the American Presidency at Hiram College. He received his PhD in political science from the University of Maryland at College Park in 1998 and his JD from Georgetown University Law Center in 1999. Among the courses Dr. Brattebo teaches are Ethics in U.S. Foreign Policy, Introduction to American Government, The American Presidency and the Executive Branch, Political Parties and Interest Groups, The Virtues, Leadership, and Legacy of Abraham Lincoln, and Engaged Citizenship. His research interests include ethical executive leadership, civic education, and globalization.

Kevin N. Buterbaugh is professor in and chair of the Department of Political Science at Southern Connecticut State University. He earned his PhD in political science from Washington University. Dr. Buterbaugh specializes in international relations and international political economy.

Sean D. Foreman is associate professor of political science in the Department of History and Political Science at Barry University. He received his PhD in political science from Florida International University in 2003. Dr. Foreman regularly teaches American government, state and local government, public policy and administration, American Political Parties and Elections, Congress, Presidency, American Political Institutions, Political Theory, Religion in American Politics, and Leadership in Public Purpose Organizations. His research interests include U.S. politics and elections, state and local government, and the politics and economics of sports.

Marcia L. Godwin is associate professor of public administration and MPA Director at the University of La Verne. Dr. Godwin received her PhD in political science from Claremont Graduate University in 2000. She primarily teaches graduate public administration courses and has extensive experience in local government administration in Southern California. Her research interests include electoral politics, civic engagement, policy, local government fiscal policies, and research methodology.

Shandra L. McDonald is a supervisor at a federal government agency. Dr. McDonald received her Doctor of Public Administration (DPA) from the University of La Verne in 2015. Her dissertation examined the establishment of the Transportation Security Administration (TSA) and the Consumer Financial Protection Bureau (CFPB) as risk bureaucracies.

Aleea L. Perry is a PhD candidate at the University of Illinois at Chicago. She expects to finish her dissertation in 2016 on work motivation and management. Her research interests include organizational studies, work motivation, state and local fiscal policies, and the intersection of politics and finance.

Ashley Skalecki is regional initiatives and partnerships coordinator for the Southwest Florida Community Foundation. She received her Masters of Public Administration from Florida Gulf Coast University where she developed her work as a graduate assistant. She currently specializes in regional grant coordination, collective impact efforts, and coalition building.

Michelle L. Wade is assistant professor in the Department of Public Policy and Administration at West Chester University of Pennsylvania. She received her PhD from Southern Illinois University in 2009. She currently teaches graduate public administration courses such as Foundations of Public Service, Public Human Resource Management, Valuing Diversity in Public Administration, Research Methods, and Staffing and Development. Her research interests focus on gender and public policy and how people construct and negotiate social identities in community organizations.

www.ingramcontent.com/pod-product-compliance
Lightning Source LLC
LaVergne TN
LVHW101448200926
848483LV00001B/92